Basic Quiltmaking Techniques

for Eight-Pointed Stars

Sherry Reis

Martingale
& COMPANY

Bothell, Washington

Credits

President .... Nancy J. Martin
CEO/Publisher .... Daniel J. Martin
Associate Publisher .... Jane Hamada
Editorial Director ....Mary V. Green
Technical Editor .... Christine Barnes
Design and
   Production Manager .....Cheryl Stevenson
Text Designer .... Kay Green
Cover Designer ....Magrit Baurecht
Copy Editor .... Liz McGehee
Illustrator ....Laurel Strand
Photographer ....Brent Kane

Basic Quiltmaking Techniques
for Eight-Pointed Stars
© 1999 by Sherry Reis

Martingale & Company
PO Box 118
Bothell, WA 98041-0118 USA

Printed in the United States of America
03 02 01 00 99 98   6 5 4 3 2 1

Library of Congress Cataloging-in-Publication Data
Reis, Sherry,
   Basic quiltmaking techniques for eight-pointed stars / Sherry Reis.
      p. cm.
   Includes bibliographical references (p.).
   ISBN 1-56477-249-7
   1. Patchwork. 2. Patchwork—Patterns. 3. Quilting. 4. Quilting—Patterns. 5. Star quilts. 6. Stars in art. I. Title.
II. Title: Basic quiltmaking techniques for 8-pointed stars.
TT835.R4534 1999
746.46'041—dc21   98-46527
                      CIP

Dedication

To my husband, Tom, who is the first to give me credit for my strengths, the last to remind me of my weaknesses, and knowing both, honors me with his enduring love.

Acknowledgments

I would like to express my true and heartfelt appreciation to:

My son, Andy, for his wonderful neck and shoulder massages when I am weary. My daughter, Nina, for bolstering me with her special late-night treats. And to both of them for being good sports when the house wasn't clean and there really wasn't anything to eat;

Carol Doak for her trusted friendship, unyielding encouragement, and smiling voice on the other end of the phone;

Sharyn Craig for happily sharing her Y-seaming technique with me and the readers of this book;

Dick and Karen Carpenter for their constant support, cherished friendship, and unfailing belief that what I do has worth;

Jamie Phillips for stitching the bindings, sleeves, and labels on the quilts in this book and especially for her sunny friendship;

Lois Ryan, the owner of the first quilt shop I ever visited, for never being a stranger and always being a friend;

Carol Clements, my friend and neighbor, for her eternal willingness to make her time mine;

Christine Barnes for her ability to edit my thoughts and words until they sparkle;

Ursula Reikes and Kathryn Ezell for their cheerful attitudes, eagerness to assist, and encouraging support;

The entire talented team at Martingale & Company, for lending their expertise to this book.

Finally, to Thumbs, for many years of joy.

MISSION STATEMENT

WE ARE DEDICATED TO PROVIDING QUALITY PRODUCTS
AND SERVICE BY WORKING TOGETHER TO INSPIRE
CREATIVITY AND TO ENRICH THE LIVES WE TOUCH.

Table of Contents

Foreword

Patchwork designs based on the Eight-Pointed Star format offer a variety of wonderful design opportunities. They can be as simple as Kaleidoscope, a basic block made up of eight wedges, or as complex as Blazing Star, a complex-looking block composed of mirror-image shapes. If you are new to Eight-Pointed Stars, you will be amazed at the possibilities.

So often, quilters shy away from these designs because they believe they are too difficult to draft or sew. Sherry will change all that for you by unlocking the secrets of this format.

When you're set to sew, Sherry will show you how to stitch near-perfect stars, with flat centers and points that meet. These techniques will serve you well in your future projects and open up new patchwork opportunities. Following the general directions, you'll find seven projects, ranging from a simple pillow to a glowing table runner and an array of impressive wall quilts—all based on the Eight-Pointed Star structure.

When you are ready to explore a bit more, Sherry's step-by-step instructions will provide you with the tools you need to create a variety of blocks derived from the Eight-Pointed Star.

This book is written in the same style as *Your First Quilt Book (or it should be!)* and the other books in the Basic Quiltmaking Techniques series. If you've worked with any or all of these books, you'll feel very comfortable taking the next step in your learning journey. If you've read Sherry's first book, *Basic Quiltmaking Techniques for Divided Circles*, you are already familiar with her easy, conversational teaching style and her simple step-by-step instructions.

I know you will enjoy working with Sherry's designs and learning all about Eight-Pointed Stars.

Carol Doak

Preface

I don't believe I know anyone who doesn't like star quilts. Quilts made from star blocks seem to sparkle, if you'll excuse the pun.

Personally, I love star designs and was drawn to them right from the start when I began quilting nineteen years ago. As a matter of fact, my very first project was a Four Patch Star pillow for my daughter. I was so proud of it!

Later, in the series of beginner classes I was taking, we were introduced to designs made using the Eight-Pointed Star, and I was in heaven. The wealth and variety of design possibilities boggled my mind. Constructing these stars of-

fered more of a challenge, but I felt ready for it. Armed with a technique for hand piecing, I learned how to accomplish this new task.

Since that early introduction, I've had the opportunity to learn various ways to piece these designs by hand and machine. Practice and experience have paid off in spectacular Eight-Pointed Star blocks and quilts.

You can't imagine how excited I am to share the techniques for Eight-Pointed Stars with you. Get ready—it's time to create star-quality quilts!

Introduction

I can still hear Jiminy Cricket singing, "When you wish upon a star … your dreams come true." All of us were mystified by stars from the time we were small. Twinkling little lights far away filled us with awe. Fabric stars offer that same feeling of amazement. Is it any wonder that star quilts are so popular?

Star patterns made using the Eight-Pointed Star technique are truly breathtaking. You may not be aware of it, but some of the designs created using this method are not stars at all. Kaleidoscope is the name of one such block.

This book is the perfect place to start if you are new to this realm of quiltmaking. Easy-to-understand text and lots of illustrations make the basics crystal clear. Step-by-step hand- and machine-stitching techniques guide you through the construction process for flat, accurate, Eight-Pointed Star blocks. Put these instructions into practice when you select and make one or more of the seven projects.

Look at the symbols on this page. You will find them time and again as you read through the information and lessons in this book. Here's what they mean:

Tip boxes include handy hints that will make a process or technique a bit easier. Read these right away!

Alert boxes let you know when you need to be careful. Your guardian angel will alert you so you don't make a common mistake. (Notice her wand!)

Down the Road boxes contain information that will come in handy on a future project, after you have more quiltmaking experience. You don't need this information right away, though, so feel free to ignore the Down the Road boxes until you're ready to explore further.

Whether this system is brand new to you or simply a refresher course, I know you'll enjoy learning the techniques for making Eight-Pointed Stars. You will gain confidence in the methods and be better prepared to make any of the projects if you read through the entire book first. You are certain to be amazed and pleased with the results. Oh, by the way, there's a star. Make a wish!

Eight-Pointed Star Terms

Eight-Pointed Star Designs: A category of designs based on eight equal 45° divisions radiating from the center of a block.

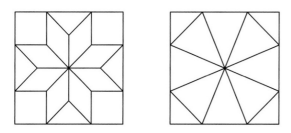

English Piecing: A piecing technique that uses lightweight cardboard cut to the finished size of each patchwork shape. You baste each fabric patch to its cardboard counterpart; then you whipstitch the basted pieces together to complete the block. Index cards are a good weight to use for your cardboard pieces.

45° Diamond: An equilateral, four-sided shape with the opposite sides parallel. The smaller angles are 45°; the larger angles are 135°.

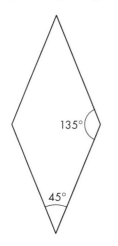

45° Wedge: An isosceles triangle (two sides are equal) whose smallest angle is 45°. This is the Eight-Pointed Star wedge.

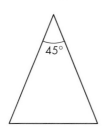

Fussy Cutting: Cutting fabric patches to display the same motif or design. Diamonds and wedges are the shapes most commonly used to fussy-cut Eight-Pointed Star designs.

Lowercase y-seam: The seam formed by joining wedge shapes in a Kaleidoscope block. "Lowercase y-seaming" is the machine-piecing method for constructing designs containing lowercase y-seams. This technique ensures flat blocks, with no lumps at the center.

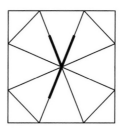

Setting in pieces: A stitching technique where a shape is inserted by pivoting at the point where three seams come together.

Y-seam: The meeting of three seams that form a capital "Y." Traditionally, set-in pieces are required in Eight-Pointed Star blocks that contain 45° diamonds. "Y-Seaming" is an updated machine-piecing method for constructing Eight-Pointed Star designs with Y-seams.

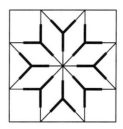

Tools and Supplies

Rotary cutter, mat, and rulers. Even a hand technician will find these tools useful for accurate, quick cutting.

Template material and permanent marker. Some templates are necessary even when you work by machine. Templates are a must for fussy cutting diamonds.

Double-faced tape. You can find this tape in office-supply and art-supply stores. It firmly holds templates to rotary rulers for cutting odd shapes with a rotary cutter.

You'll need the following tools to draft Eight-Pointed Star blocks.

Compass. There are many types of compasses, ranging from the ones we used in math class to drafting compasses to the yardstick variety. You don't need to purchase an expensive one, but your compass must reach and hold the desired setting.

Drawing rulers. These are much thinner than rotary rulers and are made specifically for drawing. Made of see-through plastic, they are marked in inches, centimeters, or are gridded. The ones marked in inches or centimeters generally start at a 0 mark that is about ¼" from the left end of the ruler, with the last inch mark about ¼" from the right end of the ruler. Even if the ends of your ruler wear slightly from normal use, your first and last inches will be accurate. You can find this ruler in most office-supply stores. The gridded ruler is a 2" x 18" clear plastic ruler marked with a ⅛" grid (usually in red or blue). The inch markings are located on each long edge. This ruler is generally available at sewing centers.

If you use a rotary ruler for drawing, accuracy will suffer. The thickness of the ruler casts a shadow, making it difficult to draw a line exactly where you want it. On the other hand, never use a drawing ruler as a substitute for a rotary ruler! You may ruin your ruler or, worse yet, cut yourself.

Mechanical pencil. This is the pencil you never need to sharpen, yet the line it produces is always the same size. A mechanical pencil really helps maintain accuracy in your drawing. Although it costs more than a wooden pencil, it won't break your piggy bank and is worth the additional expense.

Graph paper. Office-supply and art-supply stores are the places to find this drawing aid. Graph paper divided into four squares per inch (¼" graph paper) is a good size to use.

Introduction to the Eight-Pointed Star Technique

Many traditional patchwork patterns are based on the grid system. You remember this system: it divides a square into an equal number of vertical and horizontal rows to form a grid. Lines drawn within the square's grid create patchwork designs.

At first glance, you might identify the simple star design below as a Nine Patch block. Look again. Indeed, there are three divisions across the top of the block, but they are not equal. The middle division is larger than the division on each side. That rules out a Nine Patch block. Perhaps the middle section is not one, but two divisions, and is actually twice the size of the outer sections, making it a Four Patch block. If you check the measurements with a ruler, you will find that although the middle division is larger than the division on each side, it is not twice the size. So, it isn't a Four Patch block either. This is an Eight-Pointed Star.

Middle division

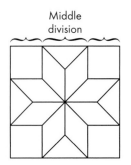

The Eight-Pointed Star is in a category all its own and is not based on the grid system. Instead, this collection of designs is based on eight equal divisions radiating from the center of a block. Each of the eight angles at the center of the square is 45°.

Here is a tip to help you recognize which designs belong to this group: The diagonal line measurement of one corner is equal to the measurement of the middle division of the block. The shape that emerges when the four corner diagonal lines and the four middle divisions are outlined is an octagon. Like a stop sign, all eight sides are equal.

Middle division

Diagonal line

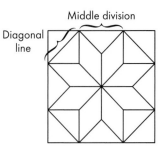

There are countless designs that fall into this classification. Each of these designs is created using the same division points. Contrary to the name, not all the designs are star patterns.

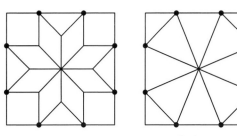

Eight-Pointed Star   Kaleidoscope

Some designs that fall into this category have divided the basic wedge, diamond, square, or triangle shapes further. The additional divisions, while creating new patterns, do not change the design classification.

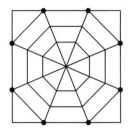

Spider's Web

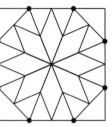

Evening Star

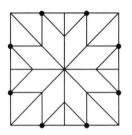

Eight-Pointed Star variation

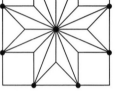

Star of the East

Certain patterns appear to lack the common characteristics of this category. Let's look at the block named World Without End. There are not eight divisions radiating from the center, no center angles to measure, and no place to check the diagonal measurement. You might not think this is an Eight-Pointed Star design, yet it is. Do the wedge shapes remind you of the Kaleidoscope pattern? If you divide this block into quarters and turn the quarters so the outside corners face in, look what you have. Now it makes sense, doesn't it?

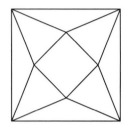 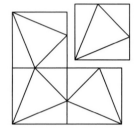

World Without End Block

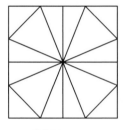

Kaleidoscope

So, as a rule of thumb, if you discover a block that:

• won't fit into any grid,

• has three uneven divisions across the top, with the middle one greater than the outer ones,

• has eight equal wedge divisions radiating from the center of the block,

• has center angles that are each 45°,

• and has a diagonal corner measurement equal to the middle division, it is likely the design is an Eight-Pointed Star. Keep your eyes open—you are certain to spy some.

Techniques for Eight-Pointed Stars

Armed with your new knowledge of the Eight-Pointed Star framework, let's see how to create star blocks. It's easier than you think, once you understand the basic techniques.

Fabric

The Eight-Pointed Star technique calls for some special considerations when it comes to choosing and using fabric.

Grain Lines

You have read that this technique is based on shapes that radiate from the center of the block. These radiating shapes are usually 45° diamonds or 45° wedges. Fabric cut on a 45° angle is on the bias, so it is not a giant leap to realize that adjoining 45° shapes will have some bias edges. We have previously learned that bias edges have the most stretch, but handled with care, they are manageable.

The 45° diamond has two sets of parallel lines for its sides. It is easy to see that if two sides are on the bias, the other two sides will be on the straight of grain. Pairing one diamond's bias edge to a second diamond's straight-grain edge adds stability to your piecing. When you cut diamonds from fabric in the same direction, this situation naturally occurs.

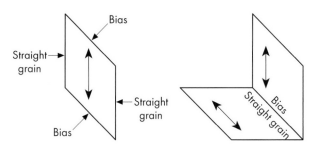

Stripes and Directional Fabric

Used in Eight-Pointed Star blocks, stripes and directional fabrics can create a pleasing, even, dynamic effect. Following are three examples of diamonds cut from a striped fabric.

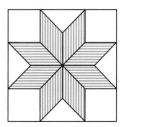
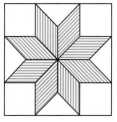

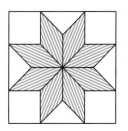

Border stripes can give the appearance of additional piecing "at no extra charge," so to speak. Look at the following block that was created using the wedge and a border stripe.

Let's turn our attention back to diamonds. The position of stripes or directional patterns will be the same in each diamond if you trace and cut half of the diamonds using the template right side up and the other half using the template reversed, or turned over. In this situation, the edges of the diamond will pair bias to bias, or straight grain to straight grain. It can't be helped.

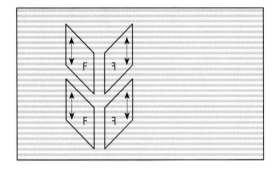

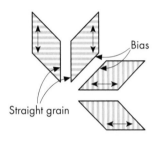

Bias

Straight grain

Strip-Pieced Fabric

Blocks like Spider's Web and the quartered-diamond units in the "Bountiful Baskets" project (page 79) can be produced in far less time using strip-pieced fabric. Spider's Web is created with wedges divided horizontally. The pairs of diamonds in the quartered-diamond units are divided vertically.

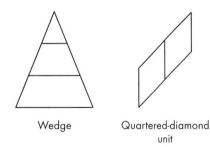

Wedge   Quartered-diamond
unit

Strip-pieced fabric works beautifully in both situations. Here's how:

Spider's Web Block

1. Cut the strips as specified in the cutting chart on page 50.
2. With right sides together, stitch the long edges of the strips using an accurate ¼"-wide seam allowance. Press the seam allowances in one direction.
3. Using the wedge template on the same edge of the strip-pieced fabric, cut eight wedges.

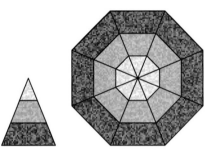

Note: For the "Spider's Web Pillow" on page 48, you will make 2 different strip sets and cut 4 wedges from each one.

If you want all wedges to be identical, place the bottom edge of the template on the same edge of the strip-pieced fabric each time, as in step 3 on the facing page. This approach wastes some fabric. You can create the look of two different wedges by cutting from each side of the strip-pieced fabric. When you piece the block, alternate the wedges. The second option uses the strip-pieced fabric more efficiently.

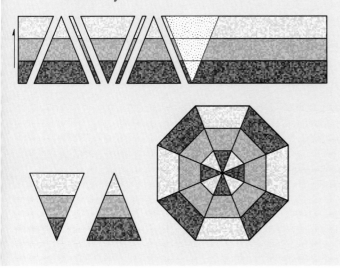

Quartered-Diamond Units

Turn to "Bountiful Baskets" (page 45) to see these units in a quilt.

1. Cut the strips as specified in the cutting chart on page 81.
2. With right sides together, stitch the long edges of the strips using a ¼"-wide seam allowance. Press the seam allowances to one side.
3. Repeat steps 1 and 2 for the second combination of strips; press the seam allowances in the opposite direction.

4. To trim the pieced strip at a 45° angle, place the 45° line of the ruler on the seam line.

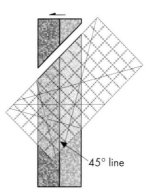

45° line

5. Attach Template U to the underside of your rotary ruler with a piece of double-faced tape so one long edge is flush with the edge of the ruler. Position Template U even with the pieced-strip edges and the 45° cut. Cut for the first unit. Repeat for additional units.

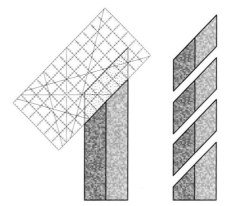

6. Join the units, one from each color combination. Place a pin through each unit at the seam for a perfect match.

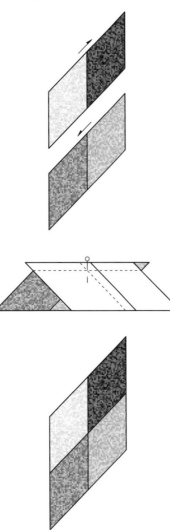

Quartered-diamond unit

Fussy Cutting

A wonderful paisley fabric is the inspiration for the Eight-Pointed Star blocks in "Victorian Stardust" (page 42). You fussy-cut the eight diamonds to display the same paisley element in the identical position in each diamond. When you join the diamonds, the center of the star holds a special view of its own. Follow the steps below to fussy-cut diamonds.

1. Trace a diamond template for machine piecing onto template plastic. (Machine-piecing templates include the ¼" seam allowance.) Trace the hand-piecing template ¼" inside the first lines. These hand-piecing lines allow you to see how the finished diamond will look. Do not trace the grain arrow. Cut out the template.

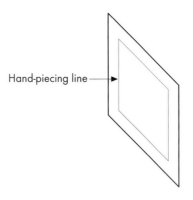

Hand-piecing line

2. Place the template on the right side of the fabric and move it until the desired design element appears within the hand-piecing lines. This is how the design will appear in each diamond. Without moving the template, trace the fabric element onto the template plastic.

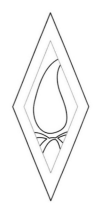

3. Match the tracing on the template to the design element in the fabric. Mark and cut as many diamonds as you need. Cut on the marked line.

If you are a hand piecer, add the pencil lines you need on the wrong side of each fabric piece. Use a sandpaper board (see tip below) to avoid stretching the edges. Smooth out the fabric on top of the sandpaper board, then trace around the template.

 To make a sandpaper board, glue a piece of fine-grade sandpaper to a file folder. The sandpaper grips the fabric, minimizing the stretch and maximizing the accuracy of your marking.

 Fussy cutting can waste lots of fabric. If the fabric you are using has more than one usable design element, why not make two or more different stars? You will need eight diamonds per star block. You'll need a separate template for each design element.

Template Tips

Included in this book are the templates needed for seven projects. The following tips will ensure that you are a happy camper, whether you are a hand piecer or machine piecer.

Trimming Template Points

The machine-piecing templates shown below have trimmed points. This detail is important. When you trim your fabric patches accordingly, it is easy to match them for accurately stitched blocks.

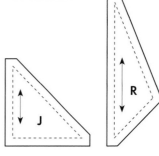

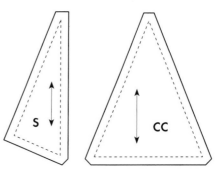

Reversing Templates

Blazing Star is the block used in the project "Star-Crossed Fancy" (page 65). You need only two templates for all the pieces in this block. Cut the fabric patches using either hand or machine piecing, with templates right side up, then reversed, right side down, to create mirror-image pairs. Be sure to reverse the templates when you trim the points.

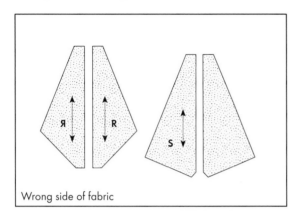

Wrong side of fabric

Okay, campers, is everybody happy? Good—it's time for star gazing!

Special Cuts

Quilting offers an array of timesaving tools, and a favorite of just about every quilter is the rotary cutter. This section reveals ways to rotary cut Eight-Pointed Star shapes.

Cutting Template-Free 45° Diamonds

Remember the first time you cut a square or half-square triangle using only your rotary equipment and no template? Were you a little nervous? I know I was. Once you cut a few pieces and learned the ropes, it turned into a simple task. You can cut diamonds "template-free" too. Here's how:

1. Cut fabric strips the width of the finished diamond plus ½" for two ¼"-wide seam allowances. (The width of a 45° diamond is the measurement between either set of parallel lines.) For example, if the finished width of the diamond is 1¾", cut the strips 2¼" wide. The edges of this strip will be the straight-grain edges of the diamond.

2. Place the 45° line of the ruler even with the bottom edge of the strip and cut along the ruler's edge.

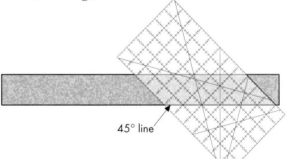

45° line

3. Turn the strip in the opposite direction. Place the 2¼" line of the ruler on the diagonal edge and the 45° line on the bottom edge of the strip. Rotary cut the final side of the diamond.

Note: The measurement for this step is under "Diamond Width" in the project cutting chart.

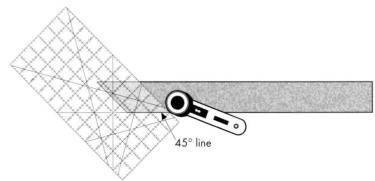

45° line

4. Repeat step 3 to cut additional diamonds from the fabric strip.

You can cut two diamonds at a time. Stack two fabric strips so the right side of each fabric faces up. Follow the above steps to cut the diamonds. Stack striped or directional fabric strips wrong sides together to cut the right and reverse diamonds at the same time.

Cutting Wedges with Templates

The wedges used in the Eight-Pointed Star technique are 45° diamonds cut in half horizontally.

When you cut wedges from fabric strips, notice how the trimmed template is positioned on the strip. Remember this placement! Notice that the straight-grain arrow runs in the same direction as the width of the strip. The strip size needed to cut wedges is the height of the finished wedge, plus ½" for two ¼"-wide seam allowances.

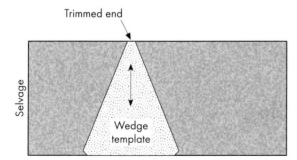

Trimmed end

Selvage

Wedge template

Let's explore a way to cut wedges by attaching the template to your rotary ruler. This technique is easy if you first cut "angled units." What is an "angled unit"? It is a piece of fabric cut from a fabric strip. The cut edges of the piece are the same angle as the wedge template, but they are parallel. You will cut two wedges from each unit.

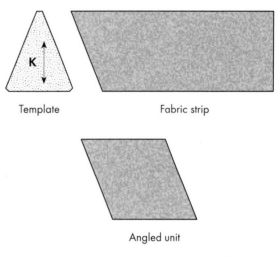

Template   Fabric strip

Angled unit

To help explain this technique, we'll use Template K (page 64) and measurements from the "Kaleidoscope Doll Quilt" (page 60). Follow the chart "Block Pieces to Rotary Cut" (page 62).

1. Cut the fabric strip 2½" wide.
2. To make the first cut, attach Template K to the underside of your rotary ruler with a piece of double-faced tape so one of the angled edges is flush with the edge of the ruler.

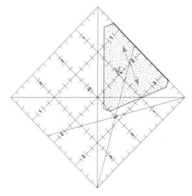

3. Place the template on the fabric strip as instructed before. Cut along the edge of the ruler.

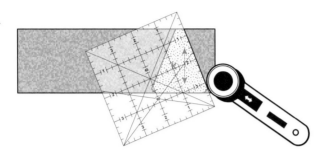

4. Turn the strip around. Remove the template from the ruler. Place the 2¾" line of the ruler on the angled edge. This measurement is the "angled-cut size" on the chart. Cut along the ruler's edge to produce an angled unit. Repeat for more angled units.

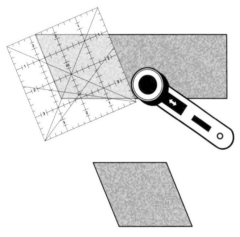

Angled unit

5. Reposition the wedge template on the ruler so the opposite angled edge is now flush with the edge of the ruler.

6. Place the template edges even with the edges of the angled unit. Cut along the edge of the ruler for the first wedge. Save the remnant.

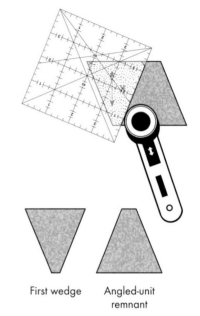

First wedge   Angled-unit remnant

7. Turn the angled-unit remnant around and cut the second wedge. Discard the waste piece.

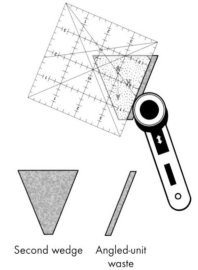

Second wedge   Angled-unit waste

8. Use Template K to trim the remaining points of the wedges.

Cutting Angled Shapes from Straight-Sided Units

Machine-piecing Templates R and S, used in "Star-Crossed Fancy" (page 65), are odd-shaped triangles. Their straight-grain arrows are parallel with the longest side of the triangle. The easiest way to cut these shapes is also from units, but the units will be straight-sided, not angled. In fact, the units will be rectangles, and once again, you will cut two shapes per unit. Follow the steps below for each template.

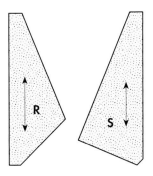

1. Cut a strip as indicated in the cutting chart. From the strip, cut a rectangle as indicated under "Unit Size" in the cutting chart. Attach the template to the underside of the ruler with double-faced tape so the longest bias edge of the template is flush with the edge of the ruler. The straight-grain arrow of the template will be visible through the ruler.

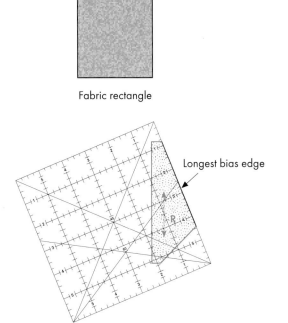

Fabric rectangle

Longest bias edge

2. Place the straight-grain edge of the template (marked by the arrow) on the long edge of the fabric rectangle, with the edges even. Cut along the edge of the ruler. Turn the rectangle remnant around and repeat. Discard the waste piece. You now have two shapes—you are halfway there!

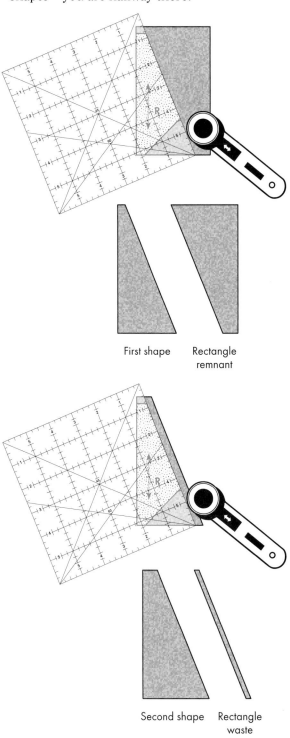

First shape   Rectangle remnant

Second shape   Rectangle waste

3. Reposition the template on the ruler, with the short bias edge flush with the edge of the ruler.

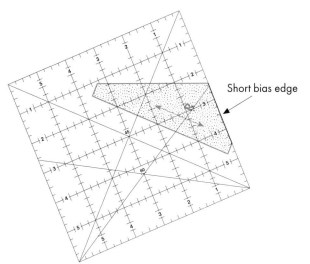

Short bias edge

4. Place the template even with the straight-grain edge and the bias edge of one fabric shape. Cut along the ruler to complete the triangle. Repeat on the second shape

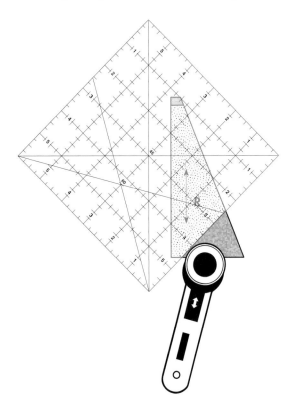

5. Remove the template from the ruler and use it to trim the points of these patches.

Work through steps 1–5 on scrap fabric as a practice run. When cutting a number of wedges, make all the step 2 cuts first, reposition the template, then make all the step 4 cuts.

Follow steps 1–5 to cut pieces Rr and Fr, but attach the wrong side of the template to the underside of the ruler as shown.

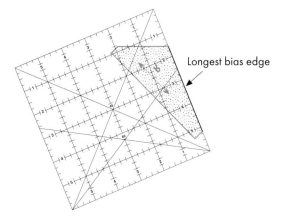

Longest bias edge

Cutting Beyond the Line

Perhaps you want to cut a fabric strip in a size that doesn't quite fall on a marking on your rotary ruler. Let's say the size is $1\frac{7}{16}$". Some of you will be able to accurately judge the mid-point between $1\frac{3}{8}$" and $1\frac{1}{2}$" on your ruler and cut strips with no problem. Many of you would prefer the benefit of a tangible line to guide your cutting. Try this technique.

1. Use a drawing ruler that has increments in sixteenths of an inch. Place the 0 mark of the ruler on the straight edge of a piece of paper, find the measurement $1\frac{7}{16}$", and mark a dot on the paper. On the same edge of the paper, repeat this step, marking several dots above the first dot. Draw a line connecting the dots; the line will be parallel to the edge of the paper.

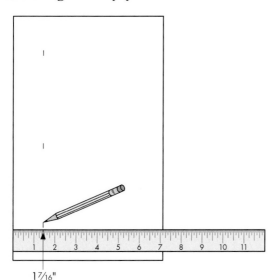

$1\frac{7}{16}$"

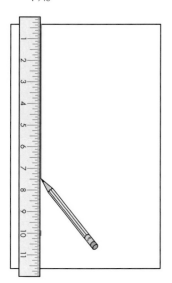

2. Turn your rotary ruler over so the wrong side faces up. Place the paper on the ruler so the pencil line is even with the edge of the ruler. Check each end of the paper for accurate placement and tape the paper to the ruler. Attach a piece of $\frac{1}{4}$" masking tape along the paper's edge. Once the tape is in place, remove the paper. The measurement you need is now marked by the tape.

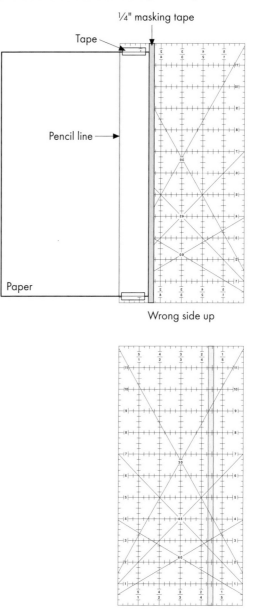

Wrong side up

Right side up

3. Turn the ruler over, position the tape along the edge of the fabric, and cut the strips you need.

Star Construction

My beginning piecing projects were constructed by hand. It wasn't a matter of choice, hand versus machine; it was simply how I was taught. The result was accurate, even though it took some time. I enjoyed hand piecing and I wasn't in a big hurry, so life was good.

Eventually, with a growing, active family, my life became more hectic and I felt the pressure to do everything faster. This included quilting, and I ventured into an area new to me: machine piecing. At first, I was somewhat disappointed because my accuracy wasn't as great as when I hand pieced. I continued to practice, however, and over time, improved my ability to produce exact, machine-pieced blocks.

The operative word here is practice! Liberace didn't play "Stars and Stripes Forever" the first time he sat down at a piano. Most likely your first star block will not be in your masterpiece quilt, but don't lose faith. Practice will build your confidence and sharpen your skills. To be honest, piecing Eight-Pointed Star blocks poses some challenges you probably haven't had to deal with until now.

Let's examine the Eight-Pointed Star and Kaleidoscope blocks to see how they are constructed.

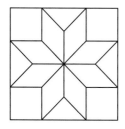 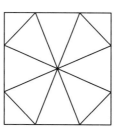

Eight-Pointed Star   Kaleidoscope

Most of the designs based on these two blocks have at least eight seams converging at the center point. That's a lot of bulk, and the opportunity for a lumpy or raised center, one that refuses to lie flat, does exist. Secondly, many of you may not have worked with designs that have three seams meeting in a Y configuration. Traditionally, the approach to this situation has been set-in pieces. Setting in means you pivot at the point where all three seams intersect, then continue your stitching. Those of you who have made a sleeved garment may recall the first sleeve you set in. Most likely the process went more smoothly the second time around. Even so, sewing a straight seam is far easier.

This chapter offers both hand and machine methods for constructing Eight-Pointed Star designs. Let's start with the technique for piecing by machine.

Machine Piecing

I was recently introduced to the best method I've ever seen for machine piecing Eight-Pointed Star designs containing Y-seams. The technique is called "Y-Seaming." This easy method eliminates the conventional set-in step, and is accurate and fast. I learned this technique from Sharyn Craig, the quiltmaker who developed it. Her method is slicker than melted butter and guarantees success.

When Sharyn introduced me to her method, she asked, "If you wanted to finish a quilt top with a mitered border, would you sew the border together first and then try to set in the center of the quilt?" The answer was obvious: of course not! "So why," she reasoned, "would you complete an eight-diamond star and set in the squares and triangles to complete it?" That makes sense, and her technique proves the point. Thanks, Sharyn, for letting me share your method!

An accurate ¼"-wide seam allowance is crucial in producing a precise block. Some machines accommodate a special ¼"-foot that will help you stitch true ¼" seam allowances. Others allow you to move the needle position until it is ¼" from the right edge of your presser foot. If neither of these choices is available on your machine, there is another option.

1. Place a small rotary ruler under the presser foot of your machine. Use the hand wheel to slowly turn the needle down to meet the line that measures ¼" from the edge of the ruler.

2. Drop the presser foot to hold the ruler in place. On the throat plate, attach a piece of masking tape or a strip of moleskin (an adhesive product available in drugstores) as a guide along the edge of the ruler. To effectively stitch an accurate ¼" seam allowance, the edges of your fabric should just touch this guide as the pieces feed through the machine.

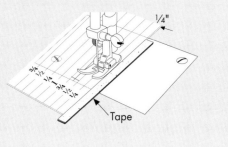

Y-Seaming

A Y-seam is the meeting of three seams that form a capital "Y." The block shown here has eight of them. Follow the steps to piece one block using the Y-seaming technique. If you prefer to work in assembly-line fashion, make stacks of the units needed for each step.

Y-seams

1. Lay out the three pieces needed for the first unit as shown (a). Flip the triangle on top of the left diamond, right sides together and edges even (b). Stitch from edge to edge (c). Finger-press the seam allowances toward the diamond (d). Trim the fabric ears even with the edge of the diamond. Repeat this step three more times.

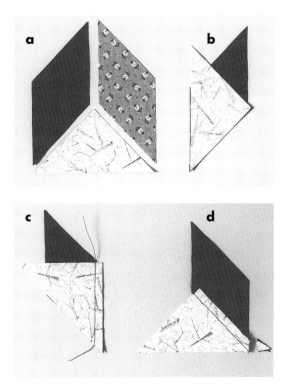

2. Position the pieces as shown (a). Flip the unit from step 1 on top of the right diamond, right sides together and edges even (b). Turn the unit and stitch from the edge to the first line of stitching and stop; backstitch to secure (c). Finger-press the seam allowances toward the added diamond. Trim the fabric ears even with the edge of the diamond (d). Repeat this step three more times.

3. Place the diamonds of the step 2 units right sides together, with edges even. Pull the triangle down and out of the way (a). Stitch from the diamond points to the previous stitching line and stop; backstitch to secure (b). Finger-press the seam allowances toward the left diamond as shown in the photo. Trim the points where you began stitching as shown (c). Repeat this step three more times.

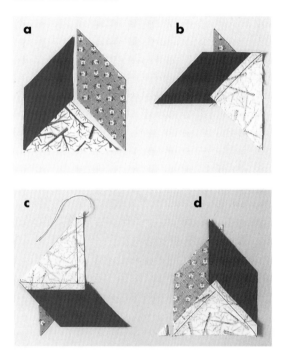

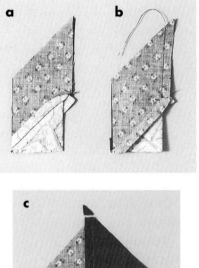

When stitching this line, it is sometimes hard to know if one more stitch will go beyond the stopping point or not. If you are not sure, stop a little shy of the point. This will not cause a problem, but stitching too far will. In this case, less is more.

4. Place the step 3 unit and a square side by side as shown (a). Flip the square on top of the unit, right sides together, with bottom and right edges even (b). Stitch from edge to edge as shown (c). Finger-press the seam allowances toward the square (d). This is a quarter-star unit. Repeat this step three more times.

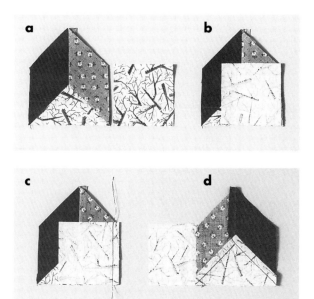

5. Place two quarter-star units side by side as shown (a). Flip the bottom unit up onto the right unit, aligning the right and lower edges (b). Turn the unit as shown. Stitch from the outside edge to the stitching line and stop; backstitch to secure (c). Be careful not to catch the edges of the diamond or square in your stitching. Finger-press the seam allowances toward the square. Repeat this step with the remaining quarter-star units.

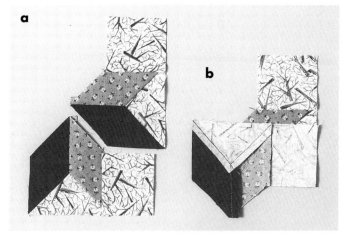

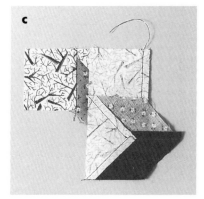

6. Fold the unit to match the diamonds of the quarter-star units, right sides together and diamond edges even. The finger-pressed edges of the diamonds will butt together for a tight fit. Fold the seam allowances of the square down and out of the way (a). Stitch the diamonds between the two stitching lines. Backstitch at both ends to secure (b). Finger-press the seam allowances in the same direction as the other diamond seam allowances. Finger-press the left edge of the square (looking from the wrong side) toward the diamond as shown (c). This is a half-star unit. Repeat this step once.

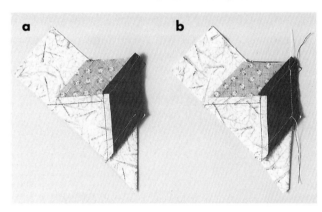

7. Place two half-star units as shown (a). Place the square of the bottom unit on the top unit, just as you did in step 5 (b). Turn the units and stitch from the outside edge of the square to the stitching line and stop; backstitch to secure (c). Be careful not to catch the edges of the diamond or square in your stitching. Finger-press the seam allowances toward the square. Turn over and repeat this step on the remaining corner.

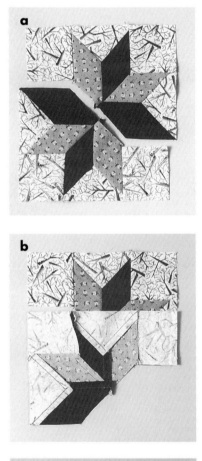

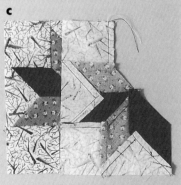

8. One more seam and the block will be complete. Place the unstitched diamond edges right sides together, matching the center points of the star (a). All the diamond seam allowances were finger-pressed in the same direction, so they will butt together for a tight fit. You may want to use a pin to hold the two halves together. Do not place the pin too close to the edges to be stitched, or it may distort the center of the star.

Set the stitch length to a longer basting stitch. Sew about a half-dozen stitches through the center of the block. Remove the pin and check for accuracy. If you are satisfied with the match, return to the regular stitch length and stitch the center seam between the stitching lines; backstitch at each end. If you are not satisfied with the match, remove the basting threads, adjust, and try again. Your block is complete (b).

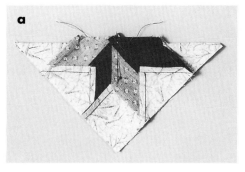

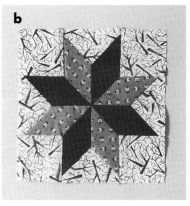

Basting is sometimes viewed as an unnecessary step in quiltmaking. Sometimes I agree, but in this case, it will save time and perhaps the block. When you baste the center, you can preview for a perfect match. The basting also holds the pieces securely for the last seam. If the match is not to your liking, you can remove the stitches easily without fear of distorting the fabric pieces. On the other hand, if your pieces become distorted, they may never fit accurately.

Finger-press the seam allowance in the same direction as the other diamond seam allowances. You will be able to press this seam so that all diamond seam allowances rotate in the same direction. This will allow the block to lie perfectly flat. Press with an iron.

For the final pressing, feel free to experiment with the seam-allowance direction on the corner squares. Changing the recommended direction may allow your block to lie flatter.

I love this technique! It is, by far, the best of any I've tried, and you can depend on the results. Even if you are a hand piecer, be brave and try it once. I am confident you will thank your lucky stars.

Lowercase y-seaming

One of the biggest selling points of Sharyn's technique is how flat the block is at completion. No lump at the center—not even a hint of one. Did you realize that in many of the steps you "stitch from the outside edge to the stitching line"? This trick allows the seam allowances at the center to remain free and flexible. If you stitched from edge to edge every time you joined another piece, you would most certainly end up with a hard, rigid lump at the center of the block.

Eight-pointed star designs like Kaleidoscope have wedges that come together in the center. Because there are no Y-seams, there are no seams to set in. For fun, I call these "lowercase y-seams." Nevertheless, there are just as many seams coming together at the center, and you don't want a lump here either. Let's apply the stitching trick to this block, too.

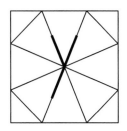

1. Place wedge 1 on top of wedge 2, right sides together and edges even. Stitch from edge to edge. Finger-press the seam allowances toward wedge 1.

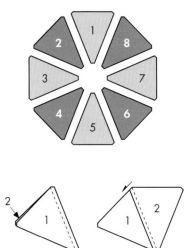

2. Place the unit from step 1 on top of wedge 3, right sides together and edges even. Stitch from the outside to the first stitching line and stop; backstitch to secure. Finger-press the seam allowances toward wedge 2. Repeat to add wedge 4. It's halfway done! Repeat the steps for the second half (wedges 5–8).

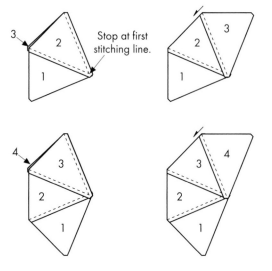

Stop at first stitching line.

3. Place the two halves right sides together, butting the seams and matching the center points; pin. Set the stitch length to a longer basting stitch and take about a half-dozen stitches across the center points. Check from the right side for accuracy. If satisfied, return to the normal stitch length and stitch from edge to edge. Finger-press the seam allowances in the same direction as the others; they will naturally fan and lie flat at the center.

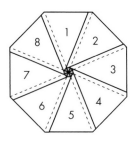

4. Add the corner triangles. Press with an iron.

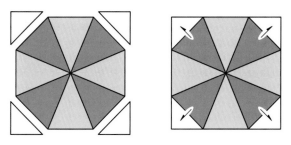

Yippee! Another accurate, flat Eight-Pointed Star block.

Hand Piecing

If you prefer to piece by hand, you can stitch your Eight-Pointed Star blocks using one of the following methods.

Traditional Star Construction

When you hand piece, your stitching begins and ends at the finished-line points. On most of these designs, you will have eight seams or more converging at the center, so there will be a lot of excess fabric there. Because the stitching stops at the finished-line points, you will be able to fan the seam allowances and the center bulk, just as you did with the Y-seaming technique, but do so carefully. Hand stitching is not as stable as machine stitching, and you don't want to stretch your fabric patches. If you do, you will end up with a center that is raised.

The traditional method of piecing Eight-Pointed Star designs has you join the diamonds, then set in the triangles and squares.

1. Stitch 4 diamonds together to make half the block. Finger-press the seams in the same direction. Repeat to make the other half.

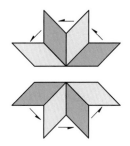

2. Place the halves right sides together and stitch to complete the star. Finger-press the seams in the same direction as before.

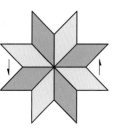

3. Stitch the triangles in place, pivoting at the inner point. Finger-press the seam allowances toward the diamonds.

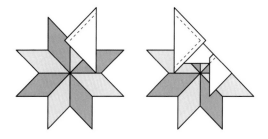

4. Stitch the squares in place like the triangles, pivoting at the inner point. Finger-press the seam allowances toward the squares.

If you decide to hand stitch the block in the traditional way, why not use the Y-seaming sequence? This will eliminate setting in the squares and triangles.

English Piecing

This is the first method I learned. It isn't difficult and the results are accurate, but it requires a good deal of preparation. However, if you find yourself on the go much of the time, this technique is portable. Why not try it once to see?

English piecing is a technique of basting the fabric patches to pieces of lightweight cardboard cut to the finished size. You then whipstitch these basted fabric pieces together at the edges to complete the block. The piecing sequence is the same as the traditional method. The cardboard stabilizes the fabric, making the setting-in step much easier. You may, however, need to bend the cardboard shapes slightly as you stitch the squares and triangles in place.

1. Make finished-size templates for your block.

2. Use the templates to trace the pieces needed from each fabric, marking on the wrong side of the fabric. Add ¼" seam allowances when you cut out the pieces.

3. Use the same templates to trace a cardboard piece for every fabric shape. Cut the cardboard on the pencil lines to make finished-size shapes.

4. Center the cardboard shape within the pencil lines drawn on the wrong side of the fabric. Place a pin to hold the two together (a). Fold the seam allowances over the edge of the cardboard and baste through all layers (b). When you reach a corner, turn the shape and continue until all sides are basted. Remove the pin (c). The seam allowances overlap each other at the points of the diamonds and triangles to form tails. Do not catch these when you stitch the shapes together.

5. Place two diamonds right sides together and edges even. Use a thread color that matches or blends with your fabrics. Whipstitch one edge, beginning and ending by taking a few stitches in the same spot to secure (a). Repeat for the remaining diamonds to make four diamond units. Place two diamond units right sides together and stitch one side to complete half the star (b). Secure the stitching at each end. Repeat for the other diamond units.

Do not catch the cardboard when you whipstitch. Catch only the fabric where it folds over the cardboard's edge.

6. Place the star halves right sides together and whipstitch the center seam. Do not catch the seam-allowance tails in this stitching. Secure the stitching at each end and at the center point. Take care to secure the center point. Otherwise, your star could have a hole.

7. Place the star right side up and place a triangle where it belongs (a).

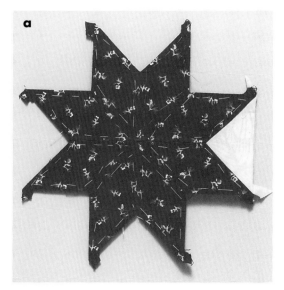

Flip the triangle so the edge matches the edge of the diamond. Whipstitch the pieces together at the edges, working from the outside edge to the inner point of the triangle. Secure the stitching at each end but do not break your thread (b).

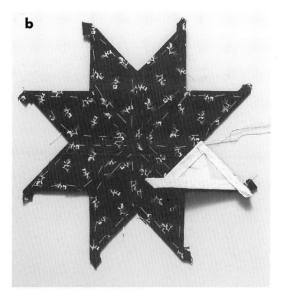

Place the adjacent edge of the triangle on the next diamond. (When you position these pieces accurately, the cardboard in some of the diamonds will naturally bend.) Secure the stitching at the inner point and whipstitch the pieces together at the edges (c).

Secure the stitching at the end. Repeat for the remaining triangles.

8. Stitch the corner squares in the same manner as the triangles to complete the block.

9. Press both sides of the block with an iron. Remove the basting stitches and the cardboard shapes. The seam allowances remain pressed open.

 If you are a recycler at heart, you will like this tip: Reuse the cardboard shapes as long as their size remains true. Discard them once the edges are worn.

 Accuracy will suffer if you remove the cardboard shapes before the block is complete.

Piecing the Flower Pot Block

Over the last few pages, you have learned a lot about set-in pieces and Y-seaming. At this point, consider yourself an official member of the Y-seam patrol!

Look at the Flower Pot block in "Bountiful Baskets" on page 79. Y-seam alert! Do you see any? Sure enough, there are five. By now, you know that when a triangle or a square meets a diamond, you have Y-seams. That accounts for three seams, but do you see the other two? The two rectangles touch the base of the basket to form two more Y-seams. Although the rectangles and trapezoids are different from the shapes you have worked with thus far, you will stitch them just as you would squares and diamonds. Here's how:

1. Join each rectangle (Y) to the flowerbasket section; stitch from edge to edge.

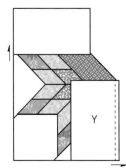

2. Stitch the angled edges of the W trapezoid and the rectangles. Stitch from the outer edge to the first line of stitching and stop; backstitch to secure.

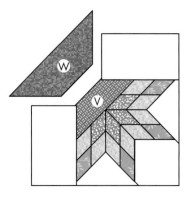

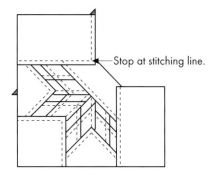

Stop at stitching line.

3. Join the seam between the V trapezoid and the W trapezoid. Stitch between the lines of stitching; backstitch to secure at each end.

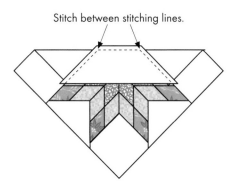

Stitch between stitching lines.

4. Add the corner triangle to complete the block.

You may have been unsure at the start, but you already knew what to do, didn't you? Y-seaming works for this block, too. I believe I see a twinkle of confidence starting to glow.

Drawing Eight-Pointed Star Designs

Learning to draw designs for your patchwork is liberating. It provides the opportunity to work with blocks in any size, without the need to search for an existing pattern. If you like the challenge of drawing your own blocks, the following Down the Road box is right up your alley. Maybe this doesn't appeal to you right now; if not, turn to page 40 and come back to this section later.

Drawing an Eight-Pointed Star design is not difficult once you understand the steps. To accommodate most compasses, I give a specific square size in the exercises. However, you can apply the steps to any size square without fail, provided your compass will open far enough to reach the necessary setting. Gather your drawing tools—compass, drawing ruler, mechanical pencil, and ¼" graph paper—and let's begin.

The Eight-Pointed Star Framework

1. Use the lines on the graph paper, a ruler, and a pencil to draw a 6" square. Draw diagonal lines in both directions to find the center point.

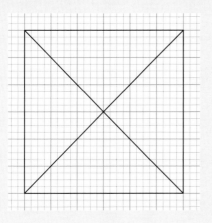

2. Place the compass point on one corner and open the compass until the pencil point meets the center of the square. Keep this setting and mark both of the adjacent side lines.

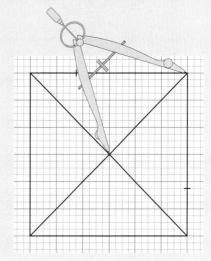

3. Repeat the above step on the other three corners. Each of the four sides now has two marks. Label the marks "A" and "B" as shown.

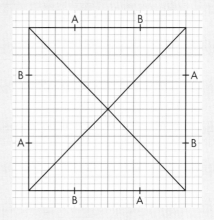

4. Draw diagonal lines to connect opposite A's and opposite B's. At the corners, draw diagonal lines to connect the B's to the A's.

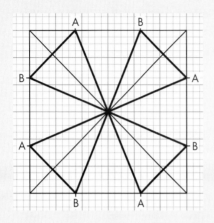

This is the basic Eight-Pointed Star framework. It is also the Kaleidoscope design. Wasn't that easy? You will need only two templates for this block: one wedge and one triangle.

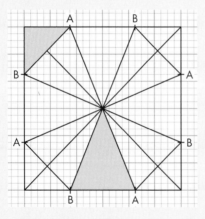

Eight-Pointed Star framework

Evening Star Exercise

This impressive block is a variation of the basic Kaleidoscope design.

1. Begin with the 6" Kaleidoscope block. Draw lines to divide the block in half vertically and horizontally. Label the four points where the vertical and horizontal lines intersect the sides of the square with C's. Label the four points where the diagonal lines meet the diagonal edge of the corner triangles with D's.

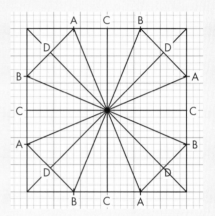

2. Draw two lines to connect the top C with each of the bottom D's. Repeat this step for the other three C's. You will need three templates for this block: the corner triangle, a diamond, and a wedge.

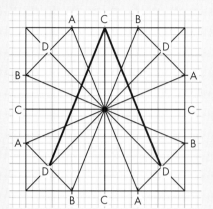

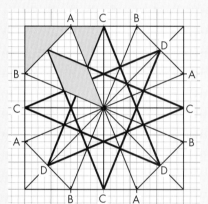

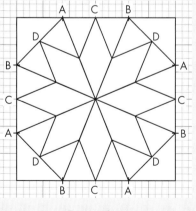

Evening Star

Star of LeMoyne Exercise

1. Follow steps 1–3 from "The Eight-Pointed Star Framework" (page 33). Also divide the square in half vertically and horizontally.

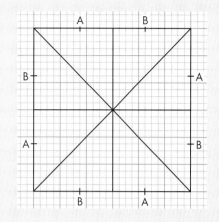

2. Draw a vertical line to connect the top A with the bottom B. Draw a diagonal line to connect the top A with the B on the right edge.

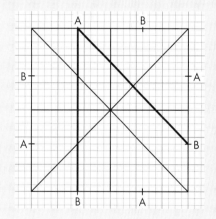

3. Turn the square a quarter turn and repeat step 2.

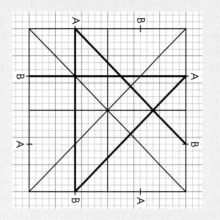

Repeat step 3 two more times. This block requires three templates: a diamond, a triangle, and a square.

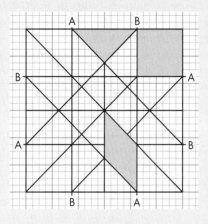

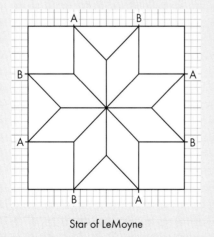

Star of LeMoyne

If we allow the diagonal, vertical, and horizontal lines to divide the squares and triangles, we create a simple star that is easy to piece. This design still requires three templates: two triangles and a diamond.

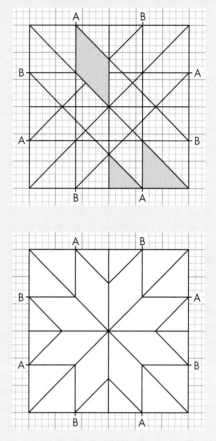

Star of LeMoyne variation

Blazing Star Exercise

1. Follow step 1 from the "Star of LeMoyne Exercise" (page 35). Label the points where the diagonal lines intersect the corners as 1's. Label the points where the horizontal and vertical lines intersect the sides of the square as 2's.

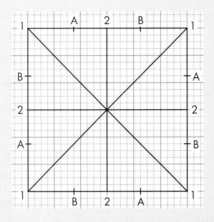

2. Draw a diagonal line to connect the top A with the B on the right edge. Draw three more diagonal lines connecting the other A's to B's as shown. These lines create an on-point center square. Label the four corner points of this square as C. Label the four points where the sides of this square intersect the original diagonal lines as D.

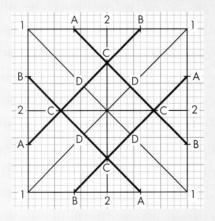

3. Draw two lines from each 1 to the two closest C's. Draw two lines from each 2 to the two closest D's.

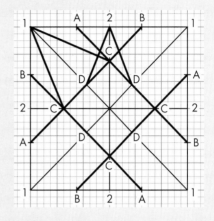

This block requires two templates, both scalene triangles (having the three sides of unequal length). You will use each template on the right side and the reverse side.

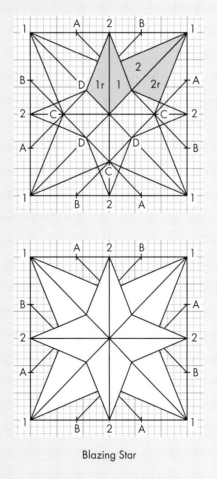

Blazing Star

Although the variety of Eight-Pointed Star designs is great, these exercises should help you draw the majority of them. Deciding which drawing steps to use for a particular pattern will become easier as you become more familiar with the technique.

Dividing the Diamond

Earlier in the book, I mentioned that the basic wedge, diamond, square, and triangle shapes are further divided in some star designs. The Spider's Web and Evening Star blocks are examples of subdividing the wedge. The simple star at the end of the "Star of LeMoyne Exercise" divides the square and triangle. Dividing the diamond can produce interesting visual effects. Let me show you several ways to accomplish this task.

Option 1

This option divides the diamond lengthwise. Simply draw a line through the length of the diamond, from the top to the bottom points.

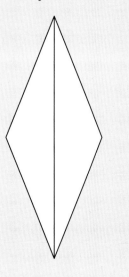

Option 2

This option divides the diamond widthwise. Draw a line through the width of the diamond, from midpoint to midpoint.

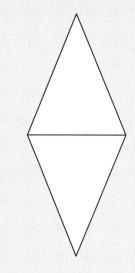

Option 3

This option divides the diamond into quarters, producing four smaller diamonds of equal size.

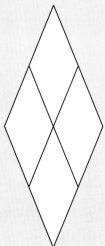

You will need to find the midpoint of each side of the diamond to divide it into quarters. Follow these simple steps.

1. Divide the measurement of one side in half. If, for example, the side of the diamond is 3", divide it by 2 to arrive at 1½".
2. Use your drawing ruler to measure and mark dots 1½" from the points on each side of the diamond.
3. With a pencil and a ruler, draw lines to connect the opposite dots.

Hooray! You did a great job! Don't worry about forgetting the steps; just refer to this section whenever you want to draw your own Eight-Pointed Star designs. Think of it as your personal ticket to the stars.

When you make templates from blocks you have drawn, remember to add a ¼"-wide seam allowance to machine-piecing templates. For hand piecing, make finished-size templates and add a ¼"-wide seam allowance when you cut your patches.

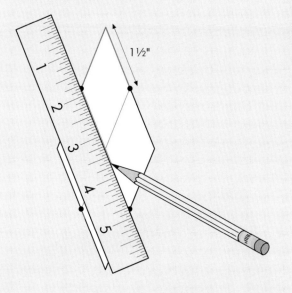

1½"

Eight-Pointed Star Projects

And now the part you've all been waiting for—the projects! There's something for everyone here, even a doll quilt. If you haven't already decided which one to make first, sit down and relax while you flip through the gallery of quilts and the instructions. Notice that each project has a materials list and cutting charts (one for hand piecing and one for machine piecing), followed by step-by-step instructions and illustrations for making the blocks and assembling the project. Pressing arrows tell you the direction to press seam allowances for a smooth, flat block.

What are you waiting for? Let's begin!

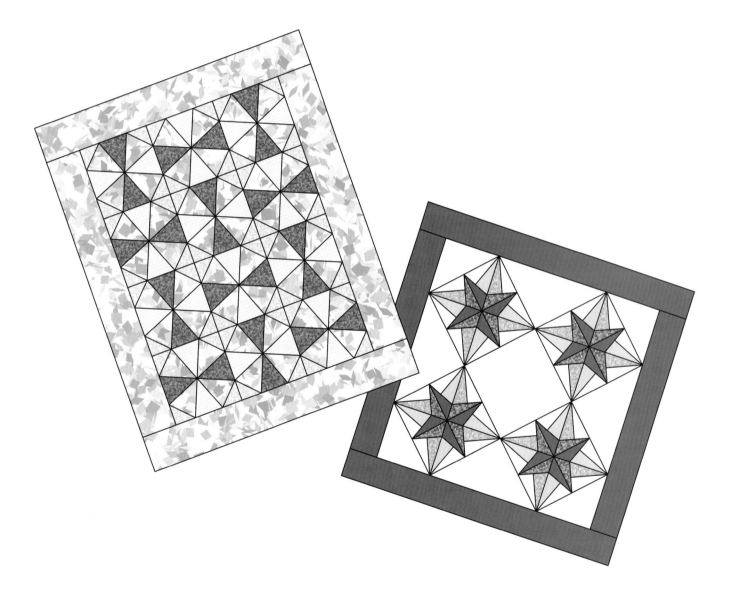

Spider's Web Pillow *by Sherry Reis, 1998, Worthington, Ohio, 15½" x 15½". The rustic colors and butterfly fabric will make you look twice to see if a spider is lurking in his kaleidoscope web. This pillow is a great beginner project. Directions begin on page 48.*

Victorian Stardust *by Sherry Reis, 1998, Worthington, Ohio, 36" x 36". Simple Nine Patch blocks alternate with fussy-cut Eight-Pointed Star blocks for an eye-catching quilt. Stars cut in the conventional way will create a countrified look. Directions begin on page 71.*

Twinkle, Twinkle, Evening Star *by Sherry Reis, 1998,*
Worthington, Ohio, 36" x 36". Evening Star and Kaleidoscope
blocks combine to create a starburst at the center of this quilt.
I think you will agree that this ambitious nine-block
wall quilt is worth the effort. Directions begin on page 87.

Simple Star Table Runner *by Sherry Reis, 1998, Worthington, Ohio, 12" x 36". Three easy-to-piece Star blocks appear to rest on pinwheels. A diamond and two triangles are the only fabric patches you'll need for the blocks. Make it for yourself or as a gift. Directions begin on page 54.*

Bountiful Baskets *by Sherry Reis, 1998, Worthington, Ohio,*
24" x 24". You can stitch baskets full of diamonds in no time when
you use strip-pieced fabric. Reproduction fabrics complete the
recipe for a time-honored look. Directions begin on page 79.

Kaleidoscope Doll Quilt *by Sherry Reis, 1998, Worthington, Ohio,
16" x 20". What a fun little quilt to make for the young lady in
your life—she might even be you! The images change from circles
to pinwheels, creating movement in this pint-size rendition.
Directions begin on page 60.*

Star-Crossed Fancy *by Sherry Reis, 1998, Worthington, Ohio, 30" x 30". This four-block quilt is the perfect opportunity to try a diagonal set. Using the same fabric in the edges of the Blazing Star blocks and the setting pieces gives the illusion of curves. Directions begin on page 65.*

Spider's Web Pillow

When learning a new technique, a pillow is a great place to start. You can cut the wedges from strip-pieced fabric, or you can individually piece each wedge. This Spider's Web pillow is a welcome sight, even if you aren't a spider! Whether you piece by hand or machine, use your machine to construct the pillow after you complete the block.

Color photo on page 41.

 Butterfly print

 Orange water-stained print

 Winter tree print

 Dark orange print

 Light fern print

Stripe

Project Information at a Glance

Finished Pillow Size:	15½" x 15½" (including the flange)
Name of Block:	Spider's Web
Finished Block Size:	10" x 10"
Number of Blocks to Make:	1
Finished Border/Flange Width:	2¾"

Note: If you machine piece this project, follow the directions for "Lowercase y-seaming" (page 28).

Materials: 42"-wide fabric

¼ yd. butterfly print
⅛ yd. orange water-stained print
¾ yd. winter tree print
⅛ yd. dark orange print
⅛ yd. light fern print
⅛ yd. stripe
12" x 12" square of muslin*
12" x 12" square of low-loft batting
12" x 12" pillow form
*This piece will be inside the pillow and will not be seen. Therefore, you can use muslin or any light-colored cotton fabric.

Spider's Web Block
Make 1.

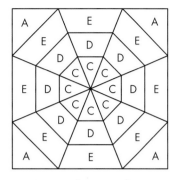

Letters indicate templates
and rotary-cut pieces.

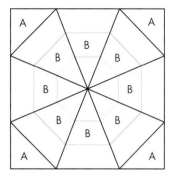

Letters indicate templates
and rotary-cut pieces
for strip-pieced option.

Cutting for HAND piecing

Setting Pieces				
Fabric	**No. of Pieces**	**Size to Mark**	**Size to Cut**	**Placement**
winter tree	2	2¾" x 10"	3¼" x 10½"	side borders/flange
	2	2¾" x 15½"	3¼" x 16"	top and bottom borders/flange

Block Pieces to Mark and Cut		

Make Templates A, C, D, and E for hand piecing. Remember to add ¼"-wide seam allowances when cutting the pieces.

Fabric	No. of Pieces	Template
butterfly	4	A
	4	E
orange water-stained	4	D
winter tree	4	C
dark orange	4	C
light fern	4	D
stripe	4	E

Cutting for MACHINE piecing

Setting Pieces			
Fabric	**No. of Pieces**	**Size to Cut**	**Placement**
winter tree	2	3¼" x 10½"	side borders/flange
	2	3¼" x 16"	top and bottom borders/flange

Block Pieces to Rotary Cut					

Make Templates C, D, and E for machine piecing.

Fabric	No. of Pieces	1st Cut	2nd Cut	Yield	Placement
butterfly	2	3¾" x 3¾"	◰	4	A

Fabric	No. of Pieces	Template
butterfly	4	E
orange water-stained	4	D
winter tree	4	C
dark orange	4	C
light fern	4	D
stripe	4	E

◰ Cut the squares once diagonally.

Cutting for Strip-Pieced Option		

If you prefer to make the wedges from strip-pieced fabric, cut the following strips from selvage to selvage across the width of the fabric. Make machine-piecing Template B. See "Spider's Web Block" (page 12).

Fabric	No. of Strips	Strip Size
butterfly	1	2"
orange water-stained	1	2"
winter tree	1	2½"
dark orange	1	2½"
light fern	1	2"
stripe	1	2"

Spider's Web Block Assembly

Lay out pieces.

If you used the strip-pieced option, the wedges are already pieced; skip to step 5.

1. Join a butterfly trapezoid (E) and an orange water-stained trapezoid (D).

2. Join the unit from step 1 and a winter tree triangle (C).

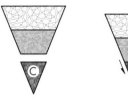

Make 4.

3. Join a stripe trapezoid (E) and a light fern trapezoid (D).

4. Join the unit from step 3 and a dark orange triangle (C).

Make 4.

5. Join a unit from step 2 and a unit from step 4.

6. Join the unit from step 5 and a unit from step 2.

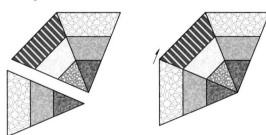

7. Join the unit from step 6 and a unit from step 4.

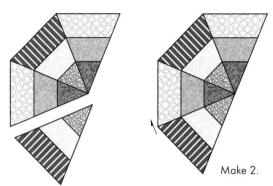

Make 2.

8. Join the two units from step 7 to complete the unit.

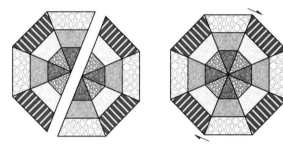

9. Add the butterfly triangles (A) to complete the block.

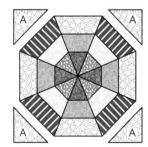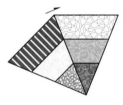

Pillow Assembly and Finishing

1. Layer the Spider's Web block, batting, and muslin square; baste. Quilt the block as desired by hand or machine, or follow the quilting suggestion.

Quilting Suggestion

2. When you complete the quilting, machine or hand baste ⅛" from the outside edge; trim the batting and the backing fabric even with the edge of the block.

3. Sew a 3¼" x 10½" border strip to each side of the block. Sew a 3¼" x 16" border strip to the top and bottom of the block.

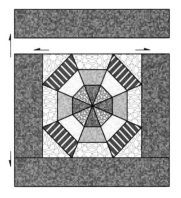

4. From the winter tree print, cut 2 rectangles, each 11" x 16". On one long side of each rectangle, turn under ½" twice and press. Machine stitch the edge.

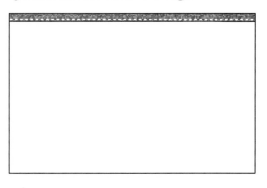

5. With right sides together, place the long, unfinished edge of one rectangle even with the top edge of the pillow top and pin. Place the unfinished edge of the second rectangle even with the bottom edge of the pillow top and pin. Machine stitch around the edges, using a ¼"-wide seam allowance; backstitch to secure. Trim the corners to reduce bulk.

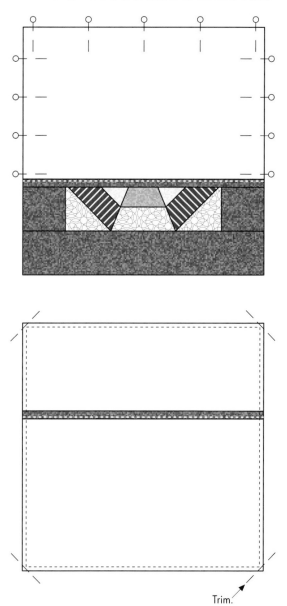

Trim.

6. Turn the pillow right side out and press the edges. Machine stitch the border 1" from the block edge to create the flange; backstitch to secure. Insert the pillow form.

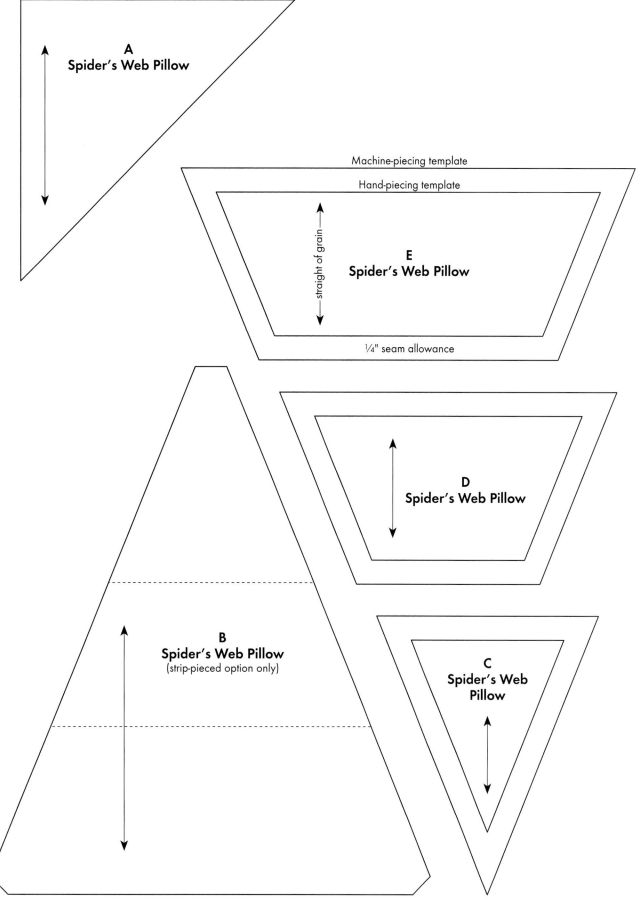

A
Spider's Web Pillow

Machine-piecing template

Hand-piecing template

straight of grain

E
Spider's Web Pillow

¼" seam allowance

D
Spider's Web Pillow

B
Spider's Web Pillow
(strip-pieced option only)

C
Spider's Web
Pillow

Simple Star Table Runner

This three-block table runner positively glows! With just two simple shapes—triangles and diamonds—you'll be creating your very own table runner in no time at all. You, too, might choose to use one of the fabulous hand-dyed fabrics available at your local quilt store.

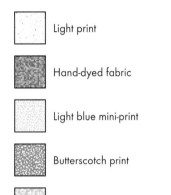

Light print

Hand-dyed fabric

Light blue mini-print

Butterscotch print

Blue sparkle

Project Information at a Glance

Finished Runner Size:	12" x 36"
Name of Block:	Star of LeMoyne variation
Finished Block Size:	8½" x 8½"
Number of Blocks to Make:	3

Note: If you machine piece this project, follow the directions for "Lowercase y-seaming" (page 28).

Materials: 42-wide fabric

⅜ yd. light print
½ yd. hand-dyed fabric (includes binding)
⅝ yd. light blue mini-print (includes backing)
¼ yd. butterscotch print
¼ yd. blue sparkle
16" x 40" piece of low-loft batting

Color photo on page 44.

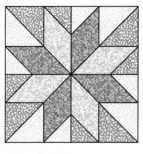

Star of LeMoyne variation
Make 3.

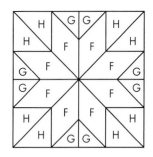

Letters indicate templates
and rotary-cut pieces.

Cutting for HAND piecing

Block Pieces to Mark and Cut		

Make Templates F, G, H, I, and FF for hand piecing. Remember to add ¼"-wide seam allowances when cutting the pieces.

Fabric	No. of Pieces	Template
light	4	FF
hand-dyed	4	I
	12	F
lt. blue mini	12 each	G and H
butterscotch	12 each	G and H
blue sparkle	12	F

Cutting for MACHINE piecing

Block Pieces to Rotary Cut		

Cut the strips from selvage to selvage across the width of the fabric. Cut diamonds from the strips. See "Cutting Template-Free 45° Diamonds" (page 16). Make Template I for machine piecing.

Fabric	Strip Width	No. of Strips	Diamond Width	No. of Pieces	Placement
hand-dyed	2¼"	2	2¼"	12	F
blue sparkle	2¼"	2	2¼"	12	F

Fabric	No. of Pieces	1st Cut	2nd Cut	Yield	Placement
light	1	9¾" x 9¾"	⊠	4	FF setting triangle
lt. blue mini	6	3⅜" x 3⅜"	◺	12	H
	6	2⅝" x 2⅝"	◺	12	G
butterscotch	6	3⅜" x 3⅜"	◺	12	H
	6	2⅝" x 2⅝"	◺	12	G

Fabric	Template	No. of Pieces	Placement
hand-dyed	I	4	setting piece

⊠ *Cut the square twice diagonally.* ◺ *Cut the squares once diagonally.*

Star of LeMoyne Block Assembly

The directions that follow make one Star of LeMoyne block.

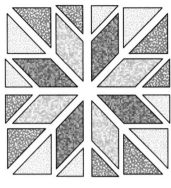

Lay out pieces.

1. Join a hand-dyed diamond (F) and a light blue triangle (G).

2. Join a unit from step 1 and a light blue triangle (H).

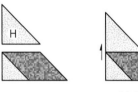

Make 4.

3. Join a blue sparkle diamond (F) and a butterscotch triangle (G).

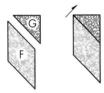

4. Join a unit from step 3 and a butterscotch triangle (H).

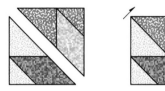

Make 4.

5. Join a unit from step 2 and a unit from step 4.

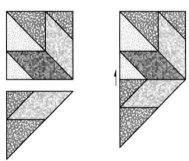

6. Join the unit from step 5 and a unit from step 4.

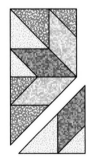

7. Join the unit from step 6 and a unit from step 2.

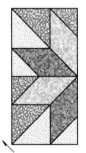

Make 2.

8. Join the two units from step 7 to complete the block.

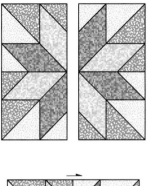

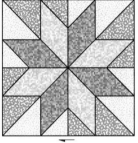

Pieced Setting Triangles

The directions that follow will make one pieced setting triangle. Join a light print triangle (FF) and a hand-dyed trapezoid (I). Make 4 pieced setting triangles.

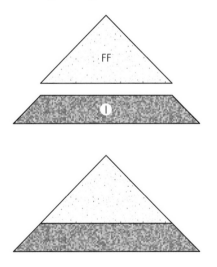

Table Runner Assembly and Finishing

1. Arrange the three blocks and four setting triangles in diagonal rows as shown. The edges of the setting triangles are on the bias and will stretch; pin carefully before sewing. Join the rows.

2. Layer the runner top, batting, and backing; baste. Quilt as desired by hand or machine, or follow the quilting suggestion.

Quilting Suggestion

3. Bind the edges.

Hand-piecing template

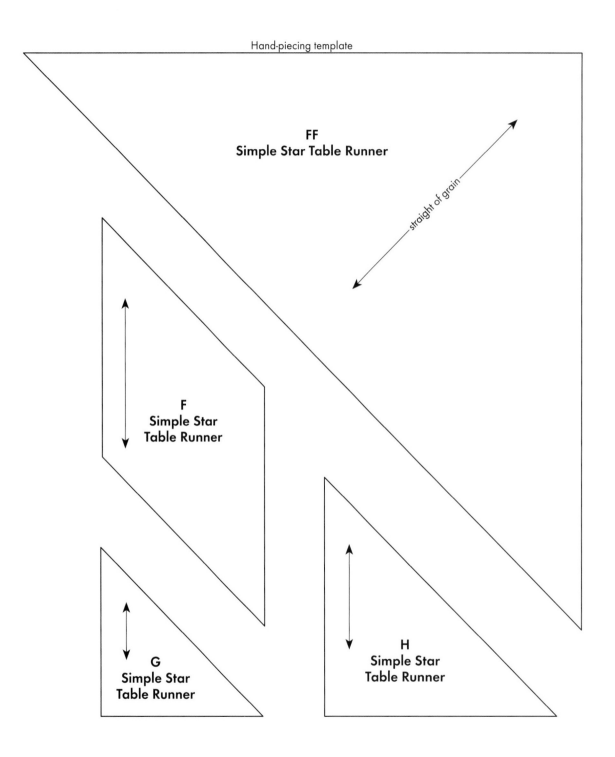

FF
Simple Star Table Runner

straight of grain

F
Simple Star
Table Runner

G
Simple Star
Table Runner

H
Simple Star
Table Runner

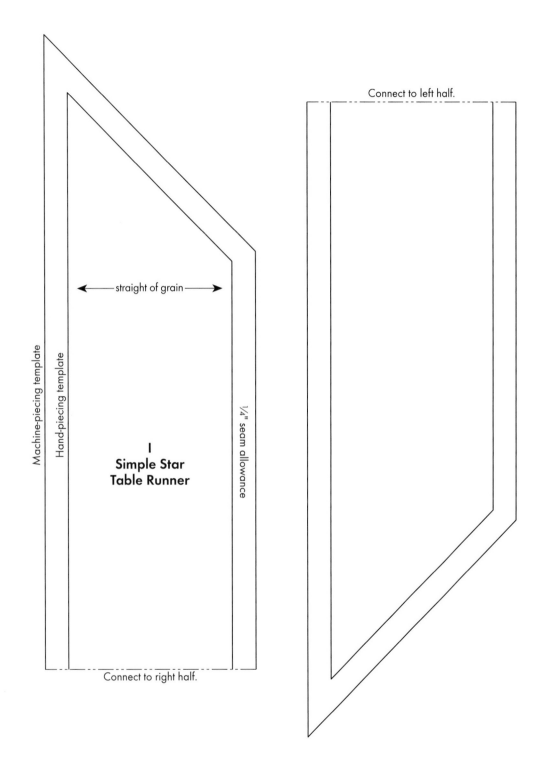

Connect to left half.

straight of grain

Machine-piecing template

Hand-piecing template

I
**Simple Star
Table Runner**

¼" seam allowance

Connect to right half.

Kaleidoscope Doll Quilt

Any little girl will smile with delight when she receives this cheerful little quilt for her dolly. If there are no little girls in your life, why not make it for yourself and wake up the little girl in you? Like every kaleidoscope, each time you look, something new appears.

Color photo on page 46.

 Bunny print

Yellow print

Light gray check

 Blue crackle

Project Information at a Glance

Finished Quilt Size:	16" x 20"
Name of Block:	Kaleidoscope
Finished Block Size:	4" x 4"
Number of Blocks to Make:	12
Finished Border Width:	2"

Note: If you machine piece this project, follow the directions for "Lowercase y-seaming" (page 28).

Materials: 42"-wide fabric

1 ⅛ yds. bunny print (includes border, backing, 6½" sleeve, and binding)
¼ yd. yellow print
⅛ yd. light gray check
⅛ yd. blue crackle
20" x 24" rectangle of low-loft batting

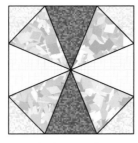

Kaleidoscope Block
Make 12.

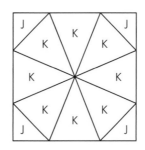

Letters indicate templates
and rotary-cut pieces.

Cutting for HAND piecing

Setting Pieces				
Cut the border strips from selvage to selvage across the width of the fabric.				
Fabric	**No. of Pieces**	**Size to Mark**	**Size to Cut**	**Placement**
bunny print	4	2" x 16"	2½" x 16½"	borders

Block Pieces to Mark and Cut		
Make Templates J and K for hand piecing. Remember to add ¼"-wide seam allowances when cutting the pieces.		
Fabric	**No. of Pieces**	**Template**
bunny print	48	K
yellow print	48	J
lt. gray check	24	K
blue crackle	24	K

Cutting for MACHINE piecing

Setting Pieces			
Cut the border strips from selvage to selvage across the width of the fabric.			
Fabric	**No. of Pieces**	**Size to Cut**	**Placement**
bunny print	4	2½" x 16½"	borders

Block Pieces to Rotary Cut

Cut the strips from selvage to selvage across the width of fabric. See "Cutting Wedges with Templates" (page 17) and "Cutting Angled Shapes from Straight-Sided Units" (page 19) before you continue. Make Templates J and K for machine piecing. Attach Template K to the ruler and cut the needed number of pieces. Remember, when cutting angled units, you make the first cut with the template shape you will be using.

Fabric	No. of Strips	Strip Size	1st Cut	Angled Cut Size	No. of Units	Template	Yield	Place-ment
bunny	2	2½"	K	2¾"	24	K	48	K
yellow	2	2⅛"		see Note below	24	J	48	J
lt. gray	1	2½"	K	2¾"	12	K	24	K
blue crackle	1	2½"	K	2¾"	12	K	24	K

Note: To accurately cut the half-square triangles using Template J, follow these steps:
1. Cut the strips into squares, each 2⅛" x 2⅛".
2. Attach Template J to the underside of your rotary ruler with double-faced tape so the longest edge of the triangle is flush with the edge of the ruler.
3. Place the remaining edges of the template even with the edges of the square; cut along the ruler for the first triangle. Turn the square remnant and cut a second triangle.
4. Use Template J to trim the points of these patches.

Kaleidoscope Block Assembly

The directions that follow make one Kaleidoscope block.

Lay out pieces.

1. Join a blue crackle wedge (K) and a bunny wedge (K).

2. Join a unit from step 1 and a light gray wedge (K).

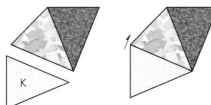

3. Join a unit from step 2 and a bunny wedge (K).

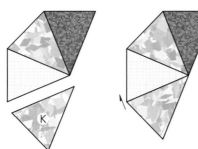

Make 2.

4. Join the two units from step 3.

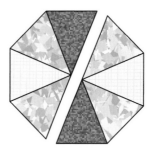

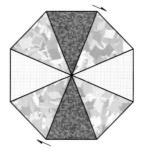

5. Join 4 yellow triangles (J) to complete the block.

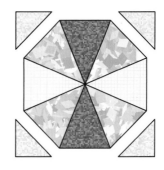

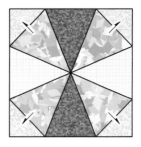

Quilt Top Assembly

1. Arrange the blocks in rows, turning the blocks as shown in the color photo for proper placement.
2. Join the blocks into rows. Join the rows to complete the quilt center.

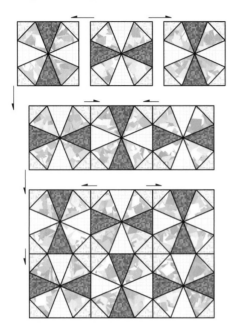

3. Add the side borders first, followed by the top and bottom borders.

4. Layer the quilt top, batting, and backing; baste. Quilt as desired by hand or machine, or follow the quilting suggestion.

Quilting Suggestion

5. Add a sleeve and bind the edges.

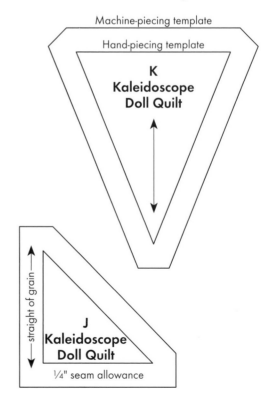

Machine-piecing template

Hand-piecing template

K
Kaleidoscope
Doll Quilt

straight of grain

J
Kaleidoscope
Doll Quilt

¼" seam allowance

Star-Crossed Fancy

Four Blazing Star blocks set on point form a dazzling display. If you use the same fabric for the edge of the star blocks and the setting pieces, your stars will float and create the illusion of a circle at the center of the quilt.

 Light tone-on-tone

 Light blue print

 Gray pebble print

 Slate print

Navy floral

Color photo on page 47.

Project Information at a Glance

Finished Quilt Size:	30" x 30"
Name of Block:	Blazing Star
Finished Block Size:	8½" x 8½"
Number of Blocks to Make:	4
Finished Border Width:	3"

Note: If you machine piece this project, follow the directions for "Lowercase y-seaming" (page 28).

Materials: 42"-wide fabric

2 yds. light tone-on-tone (includes 34" x 34" backing and 10" sleeve)

¼ yd. light blue print

¼ yd. gray pebble print

⅝ yd. slate print (includes border)

½ yd. navy blue floral (includes binding)

34" x 34" square of batting

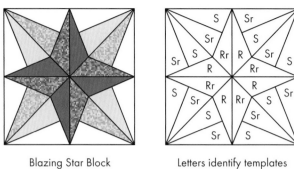

Blazing Star Block
Make 4.

Letters identify templates
and rotary-cut pieces.

Cutting for HAND piecing

Setting Pieces					

Even though you are a hand piecer, the setting pieces for this quilt are much easier to rotary cut. Once cut, mark the sewing line ¼" from the edges. Cut the border strips from selvage to selvage across the width of the fabric.

Fabric	No. of Pieces	1st Cut	2nd Cut	Yield	Placement
lt. tone-on-tone	1	9" x 9"			center square
	1	13¼" x 13¼"	⊠	4	side triangles
	2	6⅞" x 6⅞"	◹	4	corner triangles
slate	2	3½" x 24½"			side borders
	2	3½" x 30½"			top and bottom borders

◹ Cut the squares once diagonally.   ⊠ Cut the square twice diagonally.

Block Pieces to Mark and Cut		

Make Templates R and S for hand piecing. Remember to add ¼"-wide seam allowances when cutting the pieces. You must reverse each template for some of the pieces, as indicated by the "r".

Fabric	No. of Pieces	Template
lt. tone-on-tone	16	S
	16	Sr
lt. blue	16	S
gray pebble	16	Sr
slate	16	R
navy blue	16	Rr

Cutting for MACHINE piecing

Setting Pieces					
Cut the borders from selvage to selvage across the width of the fabric.					
Fabric	**No. of Pieces**	**1st Cut**	**2nd Cut**	**Yield**	**Placement**
lt. tone-on-tone	1	9" x 9"			center square
	1	13¼" x 13¼"	⊠	4	side triangles
	2	6⅞" x 6⅞"	◻	4	corner triangles
slate	2	3½" x 24½"			side borders
	2	3½" x 30½"			top and bottom borders

Block Pieces to Rotary Cut						
Cut the strips from selvage to selvage across the width of the fabric. Make Templates R and S for machine piecing. Cut the strips into units. Attach a template to the ruler and cut two from each unit for the needed number of pieces. See "Cutting Angled Shapes from Straight-Sided Units" (page 19).						
Fabric	**No. of Strips**	**Strip Size**	**Unit Size**	**No. of Units**	**Template**	**Yield**	**Placement**
lt. tone-on-tone	1	5"	3" x 5"	8	S	16	S
	1	5"	3" x 5"	8	Sr	16	Sr
lt. blue	1	5"	3" x 5"	8	S	16	S
gray pebble	1	5"	3" x 5"	8	Sr	16	Sr
slate	1	5"	3" x 5"	8	R	16	R
navy blue	1	5"	3" x 5"	8	Rr	16	Rr

◻ Cut the squares once diagonally.   ⊠ Cut the square twice diagonally.

Blazing Star Block Assembly

The directions that follow make one Blazing Star block.

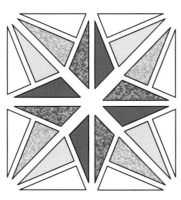
Lay out pieces.

1. Join a light tone-on-tone triangle (Sr) and a light blue triangle (S).

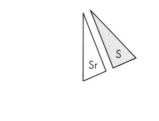

2. Join the unit from step 1 and a slate shape (R).

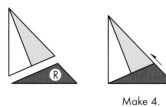

Make 4.

3. Join a gray pebble triangle (Sr) and a tone-on-tone triangle (S).

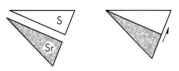

4. Join the unit from step 3 and a navy blue shape (Rr).

Make 4.

5. Join a unit from step 2 and a unit from step 4.

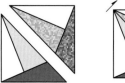

6. Join the unit from step 5 and a unit from step 4.

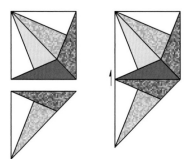

7. Join the unit from step 6 and a unit from step 2.

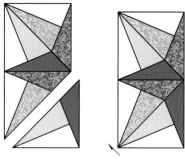

Make 2.

8. Join the two units from step 7 to complete the block.

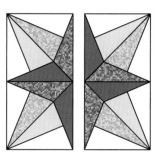

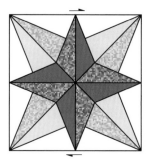

Quilt Top Assembly

1. Arrange the blocks and setting pieces in diagonal rows.
2. Join each corner section first, adding the side triangles, followed by the corner triangle. All joining edges of the triangles are on the bias, so pin them carefully before sewing. Join the blocks and corner triangles to make the center row. Join the corner sections and the center row to complete the center of the quilt.

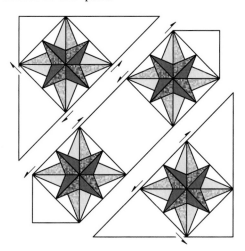

3. Add the side borders first, followed by the top and bottom borders.

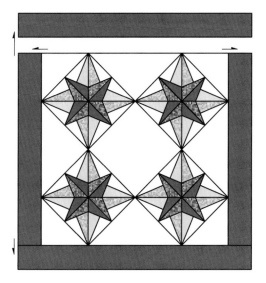

4. Layer the quilt top, batting, and backing; baste. Quilt as desired by hand or machine, or follow the quilting suggestion.

Quilting Suggestion

5. Add a sleeve and bind the edges.

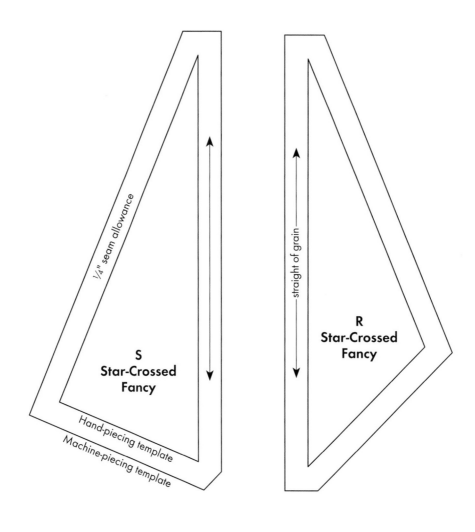

¼" seam allowance

S
Star-Crossed
Fancy

Hand-piecing template
Machine-piecing template

R
Star-Crossed
Fancy

straight of grain

Victorian Stardust

Breathtaking images develop when you fussy-cut diamonds for stars. For variety, why not make two of the stars from one element and the other two stars from a second element, as I did. You could even make each star from a different element. An inner border of the same fabric as the star background allows the stars to hang suspended.

 Paisley print

 Light blue print

Black tone-on-tone

Color photo on page 42.

Project Information at a Glance

Finished Quilt Size:	36" x 36"	
Name of Blocks:	Eight-Pointed Star	Thrifty
Finished Block Sizes:	9" x 9"	9" x 9"
Number of Blocks to Make:	4	5
Finished Inner Border Width:	1½"	
Finished Outer Border Width:	3"	

Note: If you machine piece this project, follow the directions for "Y-seaming" (page 23).

Materials: 42"-wide fabric

⅞ yd.* paisley print (includes outer border)

2½ yds. light blue print (includes inner border, 40" x 40" backing, and 10" sleeve)

½ yd. black tone-on-tone (includes binding)

40" x 40" square of batting

*This yardage is for diamonds that are not fussy-cut. If you choose to fussy-cut the diamonds (as I did for the quilt shown on page 42), you will need ½ yard for the outer border and center of the Thrifty blocks, plus whatever yardage will allow you to cut thirty-two diamonds containing the same element (or eight elements for each star). This requirement will vary, depending on the fabric's design. When buying fabric for fussy cutting, play it safe. Take your template with you when you shop and buy more fabric than you need. It's no fun to be caught short!

Eight-Pointed Star Block
Make 4.

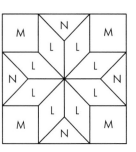

Letters identify templates
and rotary-cut pieces.

Thrifty Block
Make 5.

Letters identify templates
and rotary-cut pieces.

Cutting for HAND piecing

Setting Pieces				

Cut the border strips from selvage to selvage across the width of the fabric. Remember to add ¼"-wide seam allowances when cutting piece Q.

Fabric	No. of Pieces	Size to Mark	Size to Cut	Placement
paisley	2	3" x 30"	3½" x 30½"	side outer borders
	2	3" x 36"	3½" x 36½"	top and bottom outer borders
lt. blue	4	1½" x 27"	2" x 27½"	inner borders
black tone-on-tone	4	Q		corner squares for inner borders

Block Pieces to Mark and Cut		

Make Templates L*, M, N, P, and Q for hand piecing. Remember to add ¼"-wide seam allowances when cutting the pieces.

Fabric	No. of Pieces	Template
paisley	32	L
	5	P
lt. blue	16	N
	16	M
	20	P
	40	Q
black tone-on-tone	40	Q

*See "Fussy Cutting" (page 14) to fussy-cut the diamonds for this project. If you fussy-cut the diamonds, you may want to fussy-cut the center square in the Thrifty blocks, too.

Cutting for MACHINE piecing

Setting Pieces

Cut the border strips from selvage to selvage across the width of the fabric.

Fabric	No. of Pieces	Size to Cut	Placement
paisley	2	3½" x 30½"	side outer borders
	2	3½" x 36½"	top and bottom outer borders
lt. blue	4	2" x 27½"	inner borders
black tone-on-tone	4	2" x 2"	corner squares for inner borders

Block Pieces to Rotary Cut

Cut the strips from selvage to selvage across the width of the fabric. See "Fussy Cutting" (page 14) to fussy-cut the diamonds for this project. If you fussy-cut the diamonds, you may want to fussy-cut the center square in the Thrifty blocks, too. The following instructions are for diamonds that are not fussy-cut. See "Cutting Template-Free 45° Diamonds" (page 16).

Fabric	Strip Size	No. of Strips	Diamond Width	No. of Pieces	Placement
paisley	2⅜"	3	2⅜"	32	L

Fabric	No. of Pieces	1st Cut	2nd Cut	Yield	Placement
lt. blue	4	5" x 5"	⊠	16	N
	16	3⅛" x 3⅛"			M
	10	3½" x 3½"			P

Fabric	No. of Pieces	Size to Rotary Cut
paisley	1	3½" x 21"
lt. blue	2	2" x 42"
	2	3½" x 21"
black tone-on-tone	2	2" x 42"

⊠ Cut the squares twice diagonally.

Eight-Pointed Star Block Assembly

The directions that follow make one Eight-Pointed Star block.

Lay out pieces.

1. Join a paisley diamond (L) and a light blue triangle (N).

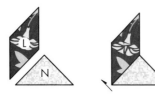

2. Join the unit from step 1 and a paisley diamond (L).

3. Join the unit from step 2 and a light blue square (M).

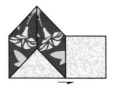

Make 4.

4. Join two units from step 3.

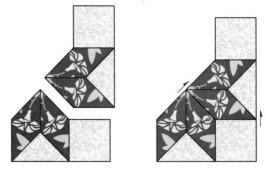

Make 2.

5. Join the two units from step 4 to complete the block.

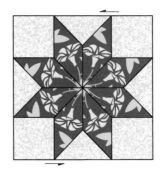

Thrifty Block Assembly
Hand Piecing

The directions that follow make one hand-pieced Thrifty block. To strip-piece this block, see page 76.

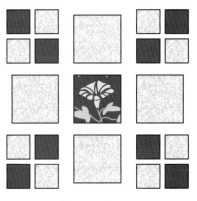

Lay out pieces.

1. Join a black tone-on-tone square (Q) and a light blue square (Q).

Make 8.

2. Join two units from step 1.

Make 4.

3. Join two units from step 2 and a light blue square (P) in a vertical row.

Make 2.

4. Join two light blue squares (P) and a paisley square (P) in a vertical row.

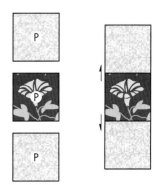

5. Join the rows to complete the block.

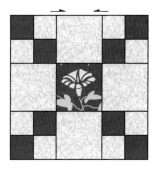

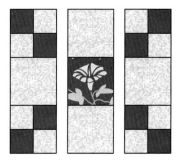

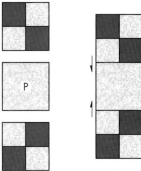

Strip Piecing

The directions that follow make all 5 Thrifty blocks using the strip-piecing method.

Lay out pieces.

1. Join the long edges of a 2"-wide black tone-on-tone strip and a 2"-wide light blue strip. The strip set should measure 3½" wide. Make 2 strip sets. Use a rotary cutter and ruler to trim the selvage end. Cut 40 segments, each 2" wide.

2. Join two segments from step 1.

Make 20.

3. Join two units from step 2 and a light blue square (P) to make a vertical row.

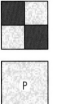

Make 10.

4. Join a 3½"-wide light blue strip to each long edge of the 3½"-wide paisley strip. The strip set should measure 9½" wide. Use a rotary cutter and ruler to trim the selvage end. Cut 5 segments, each 3½" wide.

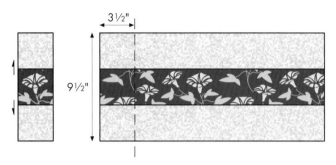

5. Join the rows to complete the blocks.

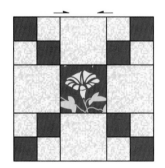

Quilt Top Assembly

1. Arrange the Eight-Pointed Star blocks and Thrifty blocks as shown below.
2. Join the blocks into rows. Join the rows to complete the quilt center.

3. Join a black tone-on-tone square (Q) to each end of the top and bottom light blue inner borders. Add the side inner borders, followed by the top and bottom borders.

4. Add the paisley outer side borders, followed by the top and bottom borders.

5. Layer the quilt top, batting, and backing; baste. Quilt as desired by hand or machine, or follow the quilting suggestion.

Quilting Suggestion

6. Add a sleeve and bind the edges.

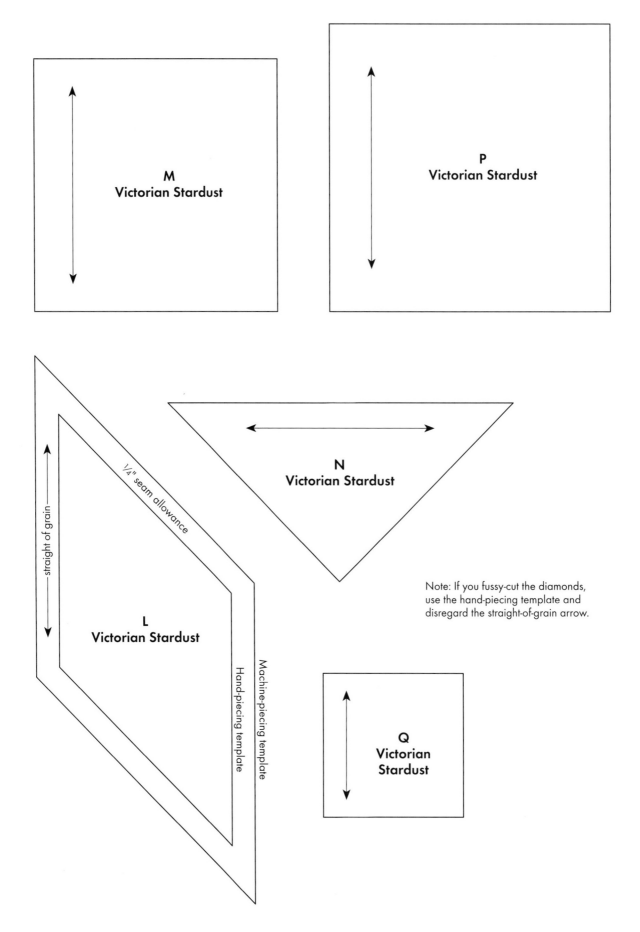

M
Victorian Stardust

P
Victorian Stardust

N
Victorian Stardust

straight of grain

1/4" seam allowance

L
Victorian Stardust

Hand-piecing template

Machine-piecing template

Note: If you fussy-cut the diamonds, use the hand-piecing template and disregard the straight-of-grain arrow.

Q
Victorian Stardust

Bountiful Baskets

These baskets are brimming with diamonds! The four large diamonds in each basket have been quartered, creating a vintage look that would surely please our quilting foremothers. Why not stitch this quilt in some of the wonderful reproduction fabrics you've been longing to use? Cut and piece the diamond units in no time using the strip-piecing technique.

Color photo on page 45.

 Light tone-on-tone

 Red print

Yellow print

Green print

 Basket weave print

Dark brown print

Project Information at a Glance	
Finished Quilt Size:	24" x 24"
Name of Block:	Flower Pot
Finished Block Size:	9" x 9"
Number of Blocks to Make:	4
Finished Inner Border Width:	1"
Finished Outer Border Width:	2"

Note: If you machine piece this project, follow the directions for "Piecing the Flower Pot Block" (page 32).

Materials: 42"-wide fabric

1 1/4 yds. light tone-on-tone (includes 28" x 28" backing and 10" sleeve)

5/8 yd. red print (includes outer border and binding)

1/4 yd. yellow print

1/8 yd. green print

1/4 yd. basket weave print (includes inner border)

1/8 yd. dark brown print

Flower Pot Block
Make 4.

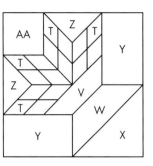

Letters identify templates
for hand piecing.

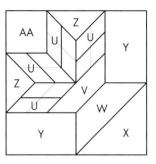

Letters identify templates
and rotary-cut pieces
for machine piecing.

Cutting for HAND piecing

Setting Pieces				
Cut the border strips from selvage to selvage across the width of the fabric.				
Fabric	**No. of Pieces**	**Size to Mark**	**Size to Cut**	**Placement**
red	2	2" x 20"	2½" x 20½"	side outer borders
	2	2" x 24"	2½" x 24½"	top and bottom outer borders
basket weave	2	1" x 18"	1½" x 18½"	side inner borders
	2	1" x 20"	1½" x 20½"	top and bottom inner borders

Block Pieces to Mark and Cut		
Make Templates T, V, W, X, Y, Z, and AA for hand piecing. Remember to add ¼"-wide seam allowances when cutting the pieces.		
Fabric	**No. of Pieces**	**Template**
lt. tone-on-tone	4	X
	8	Y
	8	Z
	4	AA
red	16	T
yellow	32	T
green	16	T
basket weave	4	V
dark brown	4	W

Cutting for MACHINE piecing

Setting Pieces			
Cut the border strips from selvage to selvage across the width of the fabric.			
Fabric	**No. of Pieces**	**Size to Cut**	**Placement**
red	2	2½" x 20½"	side outer borders
	2	2½" x 24½"	top and bottom outer borders
basket weave	2	1½" x 18½"	side inner borders
	2	1½" x 20½"	top and bottom inner borders

Block Pieces to Rotary Cut					
Make Templates V and W for machine piecing.					
Fabric	**No. of Pieces**	**1st Cut**	**2nd Cut**	**Yield**	**Placement**
lt. tone-on-tone	2	5⅜" x 5⅜"	◹	4	X
	8	3⅛" x 5"			Y
	2	5" x 5"	⊠	8	Z
	4	3⅛" x 3⅛"			AA
basket weave	4	machine template V			V
dark brown	4	machine template W			W

◹ *Cut the squares once diagonally.*   ⊠ *Cut the squares twice diagonally.*

Cutting for Strip-Pieced Quartered-Diamond Units		
Cut strips for strip piecing from selvage to selvage across the width of the fabric. See "Strip-Pieced Fabric" (page 12) and "Cutting Beyond the Line" (page 21).		
Fabric	**No. of Strips**	**Size to Rotary Cut**
red	1	1⁷/₁₆"
yellow	2	1⁷/₁₆"
green	1	1⁷/₁₆"

Join yellow and red strips for one strip set. Join green and yellow strips for the other strip set.

Make Template U for the quartered-diamond units. See "Quartered-Diamond Units" (pages 13–14).

Strip Set	**No. of Units**	**Template**
yellow/red	16	U
green/yellow	16	U

Quartered-Diamond Unit Assembly
Hand Piecing

The directions that follow make one hand-pieced, quartered-diamond unit. To strip piece this unit, see the directions below.

1. Join a yellow diamond (T) and a red diamond (T).

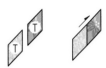

2. Join a green diamond (T) and a yellow diamond (T).

3. Join the unit from step 1 and the unit from step 2.

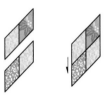

Strip Piecing

The directions that follow make one strip-pieced quartered-diamond unit.

Join a yellow/red unit (U) and a green/yellow unit (U).

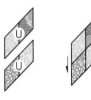

Flower Pot Block Assembly

The directions that follow make one Flower Pot block.

Lay out pieces.

1. Join a quartered-diamond unit and a light tone-on-tone triangle (Z).

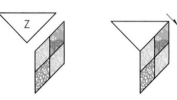

2. Join the unit from step 1 and a quartered-diamond unit.

Make 2.

3. Join a unit from step 2 and a light tone-on-tone square (AA).

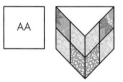
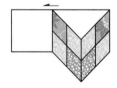

4. Join the unit from step 3 and a unit from step 2.

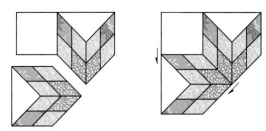

5. Join the unit from step 4 and a basket weave trapezoid (V).

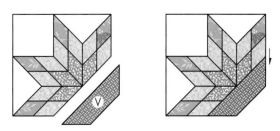

6. Join two light tone-on-tone rectangles (Y) to each side of the unit from step 5.

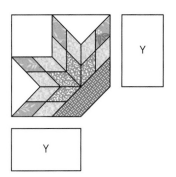

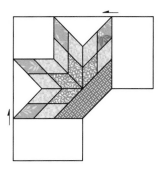

7. Join the unit from step 6 and a dark brown trapezoid (W).

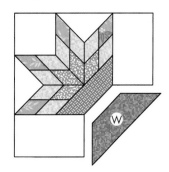

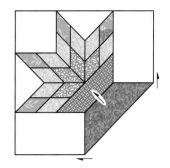

8. Join the unit from step 7 and a light tone-on-tone triangle (X) to complete the block.

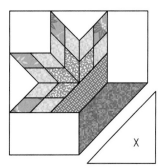

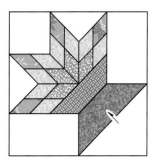

Quilt Top Assembly

1. Arrange the blocks as shown below.
2. Join the blocks into rows. Join the rows to complete the quilt center.

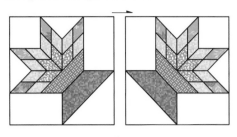

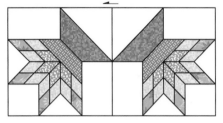

3. Add the side inner borders first, followed by the top and bottom inner borders.

4. Add the side outer borders first, followed by the top and bottom outer borders.

5. Layer the quilt top, batting, and backing; baste. Quilt as desired by hand or machine, or follow the quilting suggestion.

Quilting Suggestion

6. Add a sleeve and bind the edges.

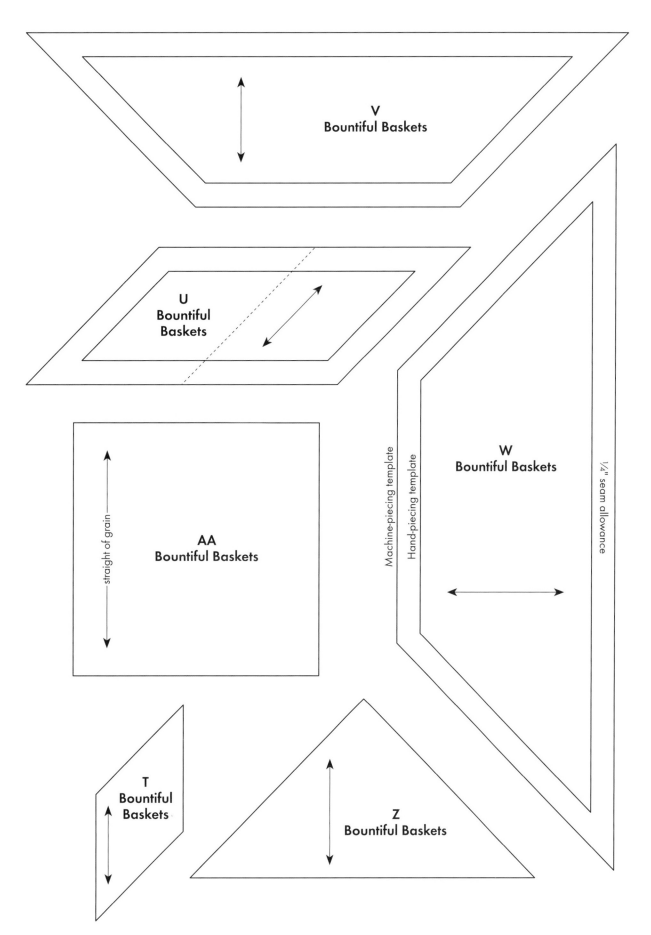

V
Bountiful Baskets

U
Bountiful
Baskets

straight of grain

AA
Bountiful Baskets

Machine-piecing template

Hand-piecing template

W
Bountiful Baskets

¼" seam allowance

T
Bountiful
Baskets

Z
Bountiful Baskets

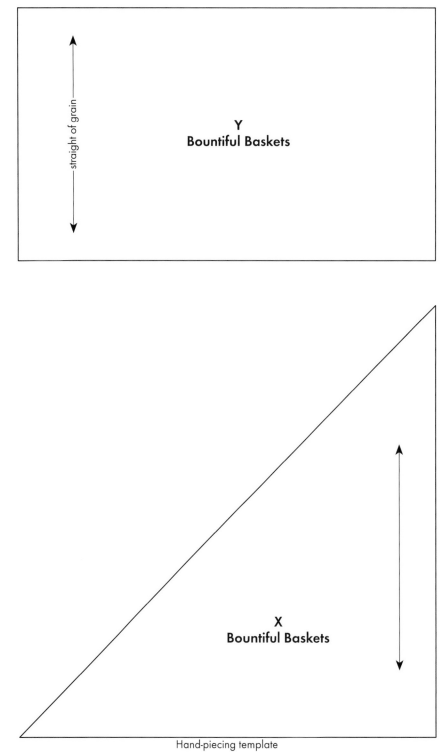

straight of grain

Y
Bountiful Baskets

X
Bountiful Baskets

Hand-piecing template

Twinkle, Twinkle Evening Star

Look at the secondary designs that spin into view in this two-block quilt. Pay careful attention to the placement of the Kaleidoscope blocks when you join the blocks to make the quilt top. The light gray wedges must face toward the center to create the secondary design.

 Light gray print

 Dark purple print

 Teal print

 Lavender print

Multicolored print

Color photo on page 43.

Project Information at a Glance

Finished Quilt Size:	36" x 36"	
Name of Blocks:	Evening Star	Kaleidoscope
Finished Block Sizes:	9" x 9"	9" x 9"
Number of Blocks to Make:	5	4
Finished Inner Border Width:	1½"	
Finished Outer Border Width:	3"	

Materials: 42"-wide fabric

1⅞ yds. light gray print (includes 40" x 40" backing and 10" sleeve)
⅞ yd. dark purple print (includes inner border and binding)
⅜ yd. teal print
¼ yd. lavender print
⅞ yd. multicolored print (includes outer border)
40" x 40" square of batting

Note: If you machine piece this project, follow the directions for "Lowercase y-seaming" (page 28).

Evening Star Block
Make 5.

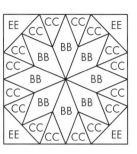

Letters identify templates
and rotary-cut pieces.

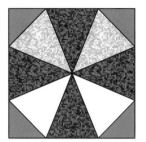

Kaleidoscope Block
Make 4.

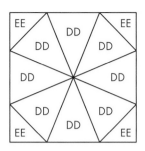

Letters identify templates
and rotary-cut pieces.

Cutting for HAND piecing

Setting Pieces				
Cut the border strips from selvage to selvage across the width of the fabric.				
Fabric	**No. of Pieces**	**Size to Mark**	**Size to Cut**	**Placement**
dark purple	2	1½" x 27"	2" x 27½"	side inner borders
	2	1½" x 30"	2" x 30½"	top and bottom inner borders
multicolored	2	3" x 30"	3½" x 30½"	side outer borders
	2	3" x 36"	3½" x 36½"	top and bottom outer borders

Block Pieces to Mark and Cut		
Make Templates BB, CC, DD, and EE for hand piecing. Remember to add ¼"-wide seam allowances when cutting the pieces.		
Fabric	**No. of Pieces**	**Template**
lt. gray	40	CC
	8	DD
dark purple	20	BB
	16	DD
teal	20	BB
	16	EE (Kaleidoscope)
lavender	20	EE (Evening Star)
multicolored	40	CC
	8	DD

Cutting for MACHINE piecing

Setting Pieces			
Cut the border strips from selvage to selvage across the width of the fabric.			
Fabric	**No. of Pieces**	**Size to Cut**	**Placement**
dark purple	2	2" x 27½"	side inner borders
	2	2" x 30½"	top and bottom inner borders
multicolored	2	3½" x 30½"	side outer borders
	2	3½" x 36½"	top and bottom outer borders

Block Pieces to Rotary Cut

Cut the strips from selvage to selvage across the width of the fabric. Cut diamonds from the strips. See "Cutting Template-Free 45° Diamonds" (page 16). Make Templates CC and DD for machine piecing. Attach a template to the ruler and cut two from each unit for the needed number of pieces. Remember, when cutting angled units, you must make a beginning cut with the template shape you will be using before cutting the needed number of units. See "Cutting Wedges with Templates" (page 17).

Fabric	No. of Pieces	1st Cut	2nd Cut	Yield	Placement
teal	8	3½" x 3½"	◹	16	EE (Kaleidoscope)
lavender	10	3½" x 3½"	◹	20	EE (Evening Star)

Fabric	Strip Size	No. of Strips	Diamond Width	No. of Pieces	Placement
dark purple	2¼"	2	2¼"	20	BB
teal	2¼"	2	2¼"	20	BB

Fabric	No. of Strips	Strip Size	1st Cut	Angled-Cut Size	No. of Units	Template	Yield	Placement
lt. gray	2	2¾"	CC	3"	20	CC	40	CC
	1	5"	DD	4½"	4	DD	8	DD
dark purple	1	5"	DD	4½"	8	DD	16	DD
multicolored	2	2¾"	CC	3"	20	CC	40	CC
	1	5"	DD	4½"	4	DD	8	DD

◹ Cut the squares once diagonally.

Evening Star Block Assembly

The directions that follow make one Evening Star block.

Lay out pieces.

1. Join a teal diamond (BB) and a multicolored wedge (CC).

2. Join the unit from step 1 and a multicolored wedge (CC).

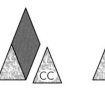

Make 4.

3. Join a dark purple diamond (BB) and a light gray wedge (CC).

4. Join the unit from step 3 and a light gray wedge (CC).

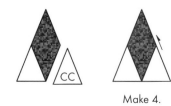

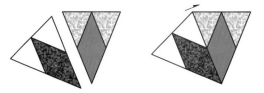

Make 4.

5. Join a unit from step 2 and a unit from step 4.

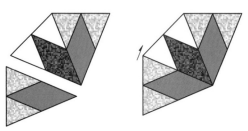

6. Join the unit from step 5 and a unit from step 2.

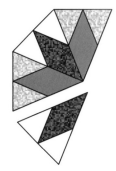

7. Join the unit from step 6 and a unit from step 4.

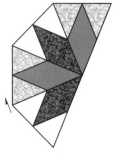

Make 2.

8. Join the two units from step 7.

9. Join 4 lavender triangles (EE) to complete the block.

Kaleidoscope Block Assembly

The directions that follow make one Kaleidoscope block.

Lay out pieces.

1. Join a dark purple wedge (DD) and a light gray wedge (DD).

2. Join the unit from step 1 and a dark purple wedge (DD).

3. Join the unit from step 2 and a multicolored wedge (DD).

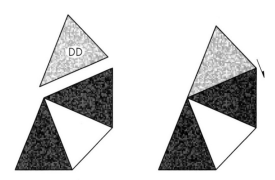

4. Join a dark purple wedge (DD) and a multi-colored wedge (DD).

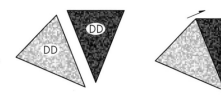 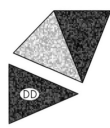 

5. Join the unit from step 4 and a dark purple wedge (DD).

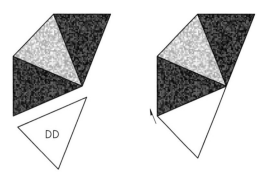

6. Join the unit from step 5 and a light gray wedge (DD).

7. Join the unit from step 3 and the unit from step 6.

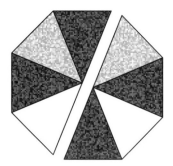

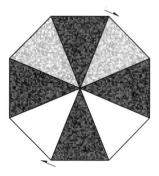

8. Join 4 teal triangles (EE) to complete the block.

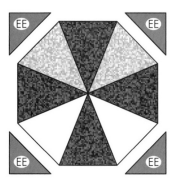

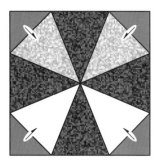

Quilt Top Assembly

1. Arrange the Evening Star blocks and Kaleidoscope blocks as shown below.
2. Join the blocks into rows. Join the rows to complete the quilt center.

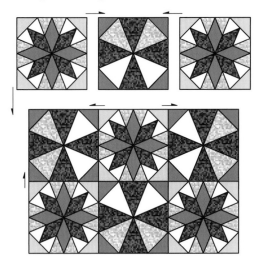

3. Add the side inner borders first, followed by the top and bottom inner borders.

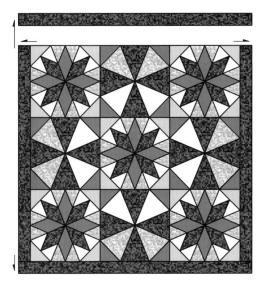

4. Add the side outer borders first, followed by the top and bottom outer borders.

5. Layer the quilt top, batting, and backing; baste. Quilt as desired by hand or machine, or follow the quilting suggestion.

Quilting Suggestion

6. Add a sleeve and bind the edges.

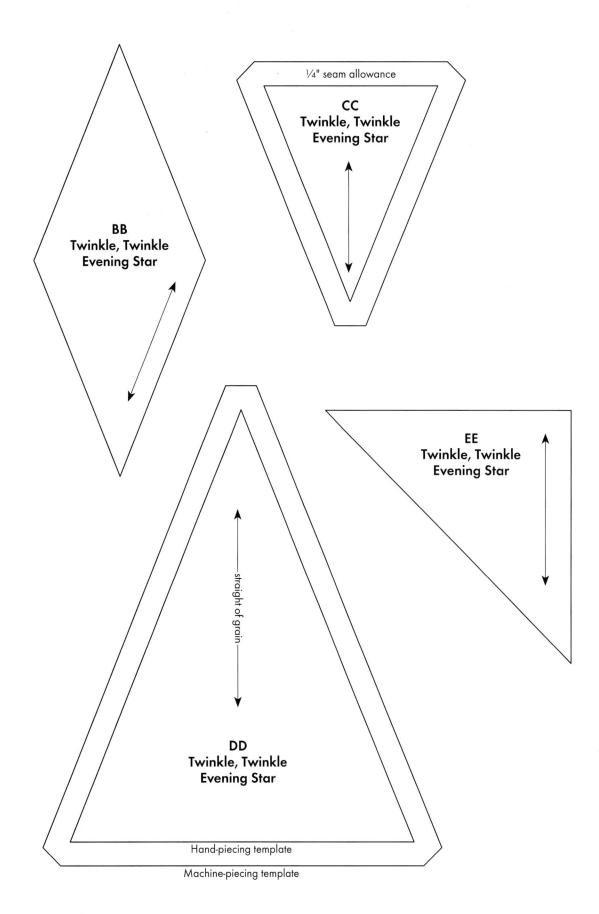

¼" seam allowance

CC
Twinkle, Twinkle
Evening Star

BB
Twinkle, Twinkle
Evening Star

EE
Twinkle, Twinkle
Evening Star

straight of grain

DD
Twinkle, Twinkle
Evening Star

Hand-piecing template

Machine-piecing template

Meet the Author

Sherry Reis learned to quilt through an adult-education class in 1979. What began as a hobby blossomed into a passion. Teaching, lecturing, and, of course, making quilts fill most of her days.

Several of Sherry's quilts have appeared in quiltmaking books and have been featured in national publications. Her first book, *Basic Quiltmaking Techniques for Divided Circles* (Martingale & Company), explores methods for making Fan, Dresden Plate, and Mariner's Compass blocks. One of Sherry's quilts graces the wall of a seniors' facility at a local hospital.

An active member of the quilting community, she is a member of several quilt guilds, where she enjoys the friendship and common bond of fellow quilters. Worthington, Ohio, is home to Sherry and her family, who are certain she owns stock in a fabric company.

Bibliography

Beyer, Jinny. *Patchwork Patterns*. McLean, Va.: EPM Publications, 1979.

———. *The Quilter's Album of Blocks & Borders*. McLean, Va.: EPM Publications, 1980.

Brackman, Barbara. *Encyclopedia of Pieced Quilt Patterns*. Paducah, Ky.: American Quilter's Society, 1993.

Craig, Sharyn. *LeMoyne Stars Made Easy*. Montrose, Pa.: Chitra Publications, 1998.

Doak, Carol. *Quiltmaker's Guide: Basics & Beyond*. Paducah, Ky.: American Quilter's Society, 1992.

———. *Your First Quilt Book (or it should be!)*. Bothell, Wash.: That Patchwork Place, 1997.

Johnson-Srebro, Nancy. *Measure the Possibilities with Omnigrid*. Tunkhannock, Pa.: Silver Star Publishing, 1993.

Books from Martingale & Company

Many of these books are available through your local quilt, fabric, craft-supply, or art-supply store. For more information, call, write, fax, or e-mail for our free full-color catalog.

Martingale & Company
PO Box 118
Bothell, WA 98041-0118 USA
1-800-426-3126
International: 1-425-483-3313
24-Hour Fax: 1-425-486-7596
Web site: www.patchwork.com
E-mail: info@patchwork.com